How Could a Loving God...?

Ken Ham

POWERFUL ANSWERS ON SUFFERING

With
Todd A. Hillard

How Could a Loving God...?

First printing: January 2007
Fifth printing: February 2011

Master Books®, Inc., P.O. Box 726, Green Forest, AR 72638
Master Books® is a division of the New Leaf Publishing Group, Inc.

ISBN-13: 978-0-89051-504-4
Library of Congress Number: 2006937545

Unless otherwise noted, all Scripture quoted is from the NASB.

Please consider requesting that a copy of this volume be purchased by your local library system.

Printed in the United States of America.

Please visit our website for other great titles:
www.masterbooks.net.

For information regarding author interviews, please contact the publicity department at (870) 438-5288.

Master
Books®
A Division of New Leaf Publishing Group
www.masterbooks.net

This work is dedicated to the sincere believer
in Jesus Christ who sees — and feels — the pain,
destruction, and decay on this earth . . . and then asks
"Why?" May the answers from Genesis to Revelation
bring perspective, determination, and tangible hope.

And to the memory of my brother Robert.

And to the memory of Henry Morris,
whose work and words transformed my life and
bolstered the faith of millions.

Contents

Foreword

BY STEPHEN HAM

If you are anything like me, you sometimes get frustrated because of your own limitations. If only I could do more than one thing at a time. If only I could be more than one place at a time. If only I could instantly access knowledge to complete any task I wanted to complete. But I am limited, and no matter how much I improve my fitness, strength, or knowledge, I am always going to remain limited to the extent of my own mortal potential — limited by power, presence, and knowledge.

Ken has written a book that is going to make you consider your limitations. Maybe you have been suffering a terrible loss or a devastating tragedy and your limitations have become all too real for you. Maybe life is going terrifically well for you and you are feeling ten feet tall and bulletproof. Either way, reality abounds, and we are one day going to come face to face with our ultimate limitation — mortality. It seems to be only when we consider such issues as death and suffering in general that we actually begin to consider our own individual mortality. As Ken deals with the subject of death and suffering in this book, you are going to have plenty of opportunities to consider your own mortality. But as I read through this book, I found a much greater subject. Hope.

As you read through these pages you are going to have a clear choice. Will you get aboard the blame train with the rest of the world or will you find the clear message of hope in a God who can save us from this tragic existence? Humanity is always looking for someone else to blame and it seems that it may as well be God. Do you notice, though, that the blame is always laid before a "loving God." How could a loving God . . . ? If your God is a God of love . . . ?

Before we read this book, I think it is important to consider the God we dare to blame. Paul describes God in 1 Timothy 1:17: "Now to the King *eternal, immortal, invisible,* the only God, be honor and *glory for ever and ever.*" Or how about Psalm 102:27: "But you *remain the same* and your *years will never end*" (NIV); Job 26:14: "Who then can understand the *thunder of his power?*" (NIV); Romans 11:33: "Oh, the *depth of the riches of the wisdom and knowledge* of God! How *unsearchable his judgments,* and his *paths beyond tracing* out!" (NIV); 1 Timothy 6:16: "Who alone is *immortal* and who *lives in unapproachable light,* whom no one has seen or can see. To him be *honor and might forever.* Amen" (NIV) (emphases added).

These are just a few verses that tell us that the God we dare to blame is eternal, immortal, invisible, glorified forever, has thunderous power, riches of knowledge and wisdom, is unsearchable in judgments, is beyond our imitation, lives in unapproachable light, and will have honor and might forever. Perhaps we'd better have very good reasons for playing this blame game. Perhaps we should think very carefully before shaking our finite fists at the infinite Creator.

It really isn't a fair fight, is it? The finite against the infinite. The limited against the unlimited.

It seems impossible, doesn't it? How do limited, mortal, finite humans even comprehend a God like this, let alone have the arrogance to blame Him for something we have no idea about? If God is unsearchable and

✝

unapproachable, how can we even bother to ask? Reading this book made me contemplate an amazing truth about God. He has revealed himself to us to save us from an impossible task of the finite finding the infinite.

Psalm 19:1 tells us, "The heavens declare the glory of God; the skies proclaim the work of his hands" (NIV). God has revealed himself to us through the work of creation. But as Ken will also explain clearly, we cannot know the mysteries of this world by looking at creation alone, especially in its current form. In Psalm 19:7, the Psalmist tells us, "The law of the LORD is perfect, reviving the soul. The statutes of the LORD are trustworthy, making wise the simple." The unapproachable God has revealed himself by giving us a written account. The Psalmist says that this account makes wise the simple. It's the ultimate instruction book for the finite. The limited now have the opportunity to understand something that the unlimited has told us. The truths in God's Word matching the physical environment we see around us has helped millions of believers to walk in a knowledge that most of this world have only dreamed of. From God's Word, it is a powerful knowledge that becomes ours, and it's ours to share.

Through the following chapters is something very special. My brother Ken will take you through a biblical study of death and suffering with the help of my brother Robert who has suffered and died and is now in the presence of the infinite God. Ken will recount some of Rob's own words that he preached on death and suffering as a Baptist pastor before entering the suffering of a cruel and fatal brain disease. You will see answers to our problems of suffering and finite limitations in this world, but you will not get them from mere mortals. They are answers from the revealed Word of the unlimited. As Ken and Rob will outline clearly, the all-knowing and all-powerful God has revealed many answers to us in His Word. When we carefully and seriously take God's Word as the authority, not only in our spiritual life but also in all matters that it deals with, we are left with eye-opening answers to the hardest questions in life. Not the least of these questions is "Why is there death and suffering?" Or if we dare to, we could be so arrogant as to ask it with a hint of blame by saying "How could a loving God. . . ?"

It is true that our limitations in this life have us struggling with mystery. We all want answers to the things we desperately want to know and we often don't like the answers we do get. We particularly hate it when part of the answer to our mystery is mystery itself. There are certainly times that we have to let God be God, and that excites no man. It is in these times that the answers God has given us create the foundation for a faith that makes us comfortable knowing that we are in the hands of someone infinitely more wise than us.

My biggest concern with books that answer questions such as these is that we walk away without asking the question most needed. While it is a good thing to study the questions relating to our life's problems, it is the answer itself that forms the most profitable question. If we can shed ourselves from our arrogant human pride long enough, perhaps we can ask it. Perhaps we can avoid, even for a short time, asking why we are suffering and contemplate why God has given us a solution. The great impact for me is that God has revealed not only the answer to our "why" question but also the solution to the world's entire problem. He is the solution. He became the solution and He remains the solution.

When you have finished reading this book, please take some time to consider a different "why" question. Ask yourself this: "*Why has an infinite God bothered to save me from a problem that I created by rejecting Him?*" This is a question that does not have you arrogantly shaking your fist from the finite to the infinite but instead has you bending your knees in tears of thankfulness and amazement.

Yes, please read this book, enjoy it, and learn from it. But at the end, please ask the right question.

God bless you as you find hope in a hopeless world.

Steve Ham

(Ken Ham's youngest brother)

Introduction

We buried what was left of Robert's body on the 12th of June in a quiet cemetery on the outskirts of Brisbane, Australia. Later in the day, we would gather with others in a public celebration of his life, but only those who were closest to him during his earthly life gathered around the freshly dug grave that morning. As the cool winter breeze blew through the forest and the Australian gum trees around us, we held each

✝

other close and sought comfort and rest in the words of the pastor and the words of Scripture.

It was the end of a long road. For months, a disease called "frontal lobe dementia" had been slowly and persistently eroding the networks of cells in his brain. For months we stood by helplessly as the disease ate away at his independence and physical presence, contorting his mind and body into a twisted, empty shell. Now, we were standing together, returning to the ground the body of our brother and friend . . . one who was also a husband and father. Standing among us was Brenda, a widow now; and pressed against her side were Joshua and Geoffrey, ages 18 and 16 at the time. There was a certain sense of relief and peace among us — and a thankfulness that his agonizing battle was now complete — but deep in our souls stirred thoughts and feelings that would not rest, echoes of questions that could not be quieted.

Why Robert? He was a good man and devoted father and husband, serving as a pastor in a Bible teaching/defending Church? Why this way? The disease had robbed him of everything that he valued most . . . his mind, his ability to communicate the gospel, his awareness of those he loved and who loved him. Why Now? Robert was only 43. His ministry, born out of sacrifice and determination, was beginning to grow. And then there were Brenda and the boys . . . boys who would never again hear the counsel and comfort of their earthly father's voice, nor would they feel the guidance and touch of his caring hand. Why did this happen when they all needed him the most?

We stood at the grave for some time, quietly, with little left to say . . . but the questions would not be silenced among us: *Why? Why? Why?*

As we wiped the dirt from our hands and said our last goodbyes, the questions hung heavy in the air. Underneath these questions was a deeper question still — a question that has perplexed mankind for ages, but was now amplified by our circumstances and our pain — and it was a question that demanded an answer: *Why would a loving God allow, or even cause, such pain, decay, and death?*

As the oldest sibling in the family, I felt the full weight of the question. How would I answer? What would I say to Brenda and Joshua and Geoffrey? I'm a Christian and I believe and love God's Word. I teach it all over the world. I preach the message of salvation and tell people about the wonderful God of love who created us; but how could I reconcile all of that with what had happened to my brother Rob? What was I to say to my mother, my own wife and children, my brothers and sisters, nieces, nephews, and so on? And what about the non-Christians who looked on and saw our Christian family struggling to cope with this

terrible disaster? What were they thinking; what were
they asking? What could we tell them in the midst of
this tragedy that would cause them to look to the God
of the Bible?

As these thoughts swirled without rest, yet another
question came up in my mind: *What would Robert say
about it all?* As a devout and gifted teacher of the Word,
what would be his answer to these questions? What would
he have said about the Bible and the God it portrays,
had he been able to understand what had happened to
him? Would he be angry? Would he turn his back on the
Word of God he so faithfully preached? What would he
say to God if he had been able to comprehend the nature
of his disease, decline, and death?

Robert's disease and illness, as you might imagine,
has been a struggle for me and our whole family. No,
there are no easy answers in one sense, but in my search
for how I should respond as a Christian, I believe that
light can be shed on this seemingly unfair, contradic-
tory, and irreconcilable situation. After all, if the God of
the Bible Rob believed in is real, and if His nature is as
revealed in the pages of Scriputure, then there has to be
a way of reconciling what seems to be so grossly unjust
with a just and holy Creator — otherwise *nothing* makes
sense.

For decades I've known and taught that the Word
of God makes sense out of confusion when it comes to

issues of history, geography, family, anthropology, morality, paleontology, etc. Since my brother's death, and the deep soul-searching it has caused, I now also know that the truth of the Word can make sense out of the deepest confusion of the heart, offering answers to the most perplexing, painful issues a person can face.

As we now turn to the infallible Word of God, may we, by His mercy and grace, be given the ability to understand the past, live powerfully in the present, and look to the future with hope, knowing that God himself has given us the answers to the questions we so desperately ask.

CHAPTER ONE

In the beginning God created the heavens and the earth. . . . God saw all that He had made, and behold, it was very good
(Genesis 1:1–31).

And It *Was* Good

The words of Genesis chapters 1 and 2 present to us the incredible chronicle of the first six days of existence. From nothing, God created the heavens and an earth. He spoke forth the first rays of light, separating them from the darkness; then He made distinction between the heavens and the waters below. Gathering the waters into seas and drying the land, God then spoke into reality plants and trees of every kind. With His voice He

✝

scattered the stars and hung the sun and moon. Filling the waters with living creatures and the skies with birds, He then filled the land with living creatures . . . and then He declared that it was "good."

But God was far from done. On day 6, God created the first two people, from whom all humanity would come. From the dust of the ground God shaped the first man, breathing life into his nostrils, and giving him dominion over everything else that had been created. Not satisfied with Adam's aloneness, he then formed a mate from the man's side, and together they began their rule over all that had been made . . . and then He declared it was *very* good.

I believe that we are incapable of imagining the perfection that existed in Eden at that time. The harmony, the beauty, the unity, the way everything worked together in peace . . . it *was* very good, but a glance at the morning newspaper or listening to the evening news makes it graphically evident that we no longer live in the beautiful world He made. Murder, divorce, abortion, starvation, and war are the norm now; devastation is common, punctuated by disasters that appear to be both natural and man-made. To get away from it all, many retreat toward undisturbed nature, but even there — no, *particularly there* — we find the world to be extremely disturbing.

Whenever I mention my homeland of Australia, people often say, "Australia is such a wonderful country." It is. It's a tremendous country. It's a wonderful country . . . compared to most others. But let's be honest; it's a rough place. We have some of the most dangerous sea creatures on the planet. Some of our sea stingers will happily kill you in minutes, and our sharks will eat you so fast that no one will know what happened to you. The bite of many of our spiders is the beginning of a slow and excruciating death. We have some of the most dangerous snakes in the world, too. Australia is also home to the most dangerous octopus in the world. If you are walking along a rocky shoreline and accidentally step on one, you'll be dead within the hour. We have the most dangerous crocodiles in the world as well (their favorite food being American tourists). We even have a deadly stinging tree! If you were to just brush up against the leaves of this tree, you would receive a painful sting that can last for years.

So imagine you've come to Australia for a vacation in order to get away from "the real world" for a while. While walking on one of our "wonderful" nature trails, let's just say you brush up against the stinging tree. The pain is so great that you rush down the hillside to the nearby ocean to wash your arm. Immediately you get stung by one of the deadly tropical sea stingers, which almost immediately makes you dizzy and delirious (not to mention the pain), so you crawl out of the ocean and fall into a nearby freshwater creek, and "chomp!" just like that you become lunch for one of our man-eating crocodiles.

Yeah, it's a wonderful country, all right. Isn't Australia a beautiful country?

I think we are sometimes very guilty of giving the wrong idea to the non-Christian when we look at nature and say, "Can't you see there's a God? Look how beautiful this world is? Can't you see there's a God?" And they're looking out there and you know what they are seeing? They're seeing people dying, they're seeing tragedies, they're seeing suffering, they're seeing death, they're seeing disease — and they don't see a beautiful world.

I even think we are sometimes giving the wrong message to our kids through most of our Sunday school literature. When we want to talk to kids about God being "the great Designer" or "the great Creator," we often turn to nature as an example of His creative "beauty." Look at the pictures you see in the Sunday school books and in Christian school textbooks, aren't they "beautiful"? Sure, look how God beautifully designed this little fox to rip the insides out of the bunny! See the dinosaur bones? Yeah, his body was crushed under the weight of tons of sediment. Look how that mosquito sucks the blood out of that little fawn!

We point at nature and life and teach our kids to sing "All things bright and beautiful! The Lord God made them all!" In reality, maybe we should be teaching them to sing "All things maimed and mangled! The Lord God cursed them all!"

A friend of mine lived in the mountains near the coast south of Brisbane. He said, "I take my non-Christian friends up on the mountain here, and we look over this beautiful countryside and the beach and I say, 'Can't you see there's a God? Look at the beautiful world He made!' " I differ with him. What we see in Australia is not the world that He made — and it's only beautiful compared to other countries! At those beaches around Brisbane, you're liable to have the blue ringed octopus and sea stingers bring an abrupt end to your beautiful afternoon outing.

No, it's not a beautiful world; it's a dangerous and deadly one. In Australia, even the Sprint phone company understands this. They have advertisements around Australia to remind you to call home . . . so people know you're still alive. (Actually, I thought it was a pretty great ad really; playing off the fact that it's not a wonderful world anymore.)

In nature, we do see a *remnant* of beauty, a shattered reflection of the original perfection of Eden. But it's all in the context of death and destruction . . . *all* of it. Take the Grand Canyon, for example. If you took a non-Christian to this magnificent place — and it is magnificent, by the way; the views are indescribable, particularly at sunrise and sunset — and the two of you were sitting on the edge of the mile-deep canyon, and you say to your friend, "Can't you see there is a God of love in the beauty of what He has created?" Would that be an accurate lead in to a spiritual conversation? Is nature really an illustration of His love?

Certainly there is a beauty there, but it's *not* an expression of love. The Grand Canyon is residue from a cataclysmic act of God's judgment, a violent worldwide flood that tore into the earth and entombed billions of living organisms. That's the *real* bigger picture, and to communicate something else to a non-believer isn't communicating biblical Christianity.

I remember being in the British Museum in London. It's an impressive place. The Museum of Natural History is filled with excellent dinosaur specimens as well as the Darwin exhibit. Then they have the British Museum of Art. It too is filled with an impressive collection of statues and artifacts that the British have ripped off from around the world over the years. I was watching a group looking at one of the statues from ancient Greece. It was missing part of the head, both arms, and part of the torso. Still it stood tall, the white marble shining in the light. People were looking at it, saying, "Wonderful!" "Inspiring!" "Beautiful!" But a little boy nearby said, "What are you talking about? It looks all broken to me!"

Both observations were correct, of course. The adults could imagine the beauty in the fact that a tremendously talented sculptor had, at one time, captured the wonder of the human physique in stone . . . but the boy saw it for what it was today: a chunk of worn, shattered, and incomplete rock. And you know, it is really the same with this earth. How many times do we as people look at this earth and say, "Look at this beautiful world and the trees and the birds and look at the other animals and isn't that a beautiful world that God made?" Well I've got news for you: It all looks broken to me. It's a broken world. And when we use nature as an example of God's beauty and love, we are giving the wrong idea.

The movie *Madagascar* does a great job of playing off of this. (That's a great movie, by the way; very funny.) At one point all these animals are skipping through the forest. They've recently escaped from the zoo to find a better life in the wild. As they meander through the woods, the song "What a Wonderful World" by Louie Armstrong is playing in the background . . . but every time they turn around, an animal jumps out of the bushes and grabs some cute little furry creature and rips its head off, or swallows it, or puts the squeeze on it.

The irony is hysterical. Sure, it's very funny in an animated movie like *Madagascar,* but it's not so funny when it's in your own neighborhood, or in your own family. This world is filled with disease, destruction, decay, and death . . . and when it comes to our home, the ramifications can spread like shock waves through every aspect of our being.

Facing Reality

On the telephone 10,000 miles away, my sister was trying to describe my brother's physical appearance. "Do you remember the TV programs that showed those horrible pictures of prisoners from the concentration camps?" she asked. "Remember how thin they looked from starvation? Ken, in a way, Robert reminds me of them." I tried to imagine it; then, as the image appeared in my mind, I tried to *not* imagine it. All I knew was that I wanted to see my younger brother at least one more time. He was so young — early forties — how could this be happening to him? I boarded a plane for 20 hours of flying, giving me lots of time to reflect on the past and contemplate the future.

A few hours after arriving in Australia, I walked into the nursing home with my mother. My visit was a surprise for her, but our joyful reunion quickly dissolved into tears as Mother conveyed what had taken place the last several weeks. I hadn't seen Robert for a few months and I knew that no matter how hard I tried, I would not be prepared for what I was about to experience.

My heart began to race as we walked the corridors of the nursing home. It was a pathetic sight. In one large area, a dozen or so mostly elderly people sat in silence, gazing into nowhere. One lady whistled continually while another kept saying certain words over and over again. Periodic groans were heard from a man in the corner, and beside him another lady kept moving her legs and body in a peculiar continual motion. Some sat motionless, their contorted faces and glassy eyes glued on the television. Only one person seemed aware of my presence, but when he spoke, the words were fragmented and unintelligible.

Inside, my heart was breaking. I was looking at someone's wife and mother, a husband and father, a son or daughter. On the walls hung pictures of some of these people — images of life before the horrible sicknesses overtook them. The contrast was so stark it was hard to believe I was looking at the same people.

This was a Christian nursing home. Most of these patients were dedicated Believers — Sunday school teachers, deacons, and devoted parents. One 78-year-old man in a room nearby had been an active evangelist. His family was gathered around him as he was breathing his last after a seven-year battle with Alzheimer's disease.

Then I saw Robert. He was lying there, hardly moving. He showed very little (if any) signs of recognition of his mother and eldest brother. Mum tenderly stroked his forehead and then began the arduous task of trying to get him to swallow a special drink she had prepared for him. Increasingly, his swallowing ability was disappearing. His food had to be put through a blender and fed to him teaspoon by teaspoon or through a drinking cup.

✝

He would swallow and then choke; swallow and then choke. Mum would wipe his face and wait to give him another sip. At times, tears would run down her face. She was so patient and so loving, talking to him and caring for him just as one would for a baby. At times, we both held his hands. He would look at us, and once or twice I wondered whether I saw a flash of recognition in his facial expressions — and then it was gone.

Yes, when disease, destruction, decay, or death come "home," it's time for a difficult reality check. In those hours we stare life — *real* life — in the eyes, and face issues that can often be avoided in the course of normal life. Perhaps you've been there too. Maybe you're there now, facing the bitter realities of life. Even if you haven't, make no mistake, you *will* face these realities soon enough — and with the reality comes questions.

The Question

The issues of suffering and death beg one of the most perplexing and pressing questions that's being asked in our culture: "How can there be a God of love if there is always death and suffering in the world?" The question is far from hypothetical or philosophical; it's both theological and highly practical . . . and it's usually asked when we face what appears to be a tragic inconsistency in the world.

After the tidal wave hit Indonesia, many asked how could there be a God of love. *Look at the masses of poor and struggling who were pulled back into the sea.* A man ignites a truck bomb outside of a federal building in Oklahoma. The collapsing building crushes a day care center filled with children. *Where was God when that happened?* What about the wars? What about the Holocaust? I mean, how *could* there be a God of love?

The Christian believes that God is love, that God cares, that He is present everywhere, and that He is all-powerful. We believe that He knows everything and is merciful and forgiving. We believe that God created the universe and everything in it, declaring that it was "very good." And yet even superficial observations indicate we've got some "problems." How do we reconcile what we see and what we believe as Christians?

We see what happened on 9/11 in New York. We look at massive famine in Africa. We hear of girls suffering at the hands of their own fathers in our own neighborhoods. Just think about death in general (let alone the death of those who are young and "innocent"). It doesn't seem right at all and people get angry at God over these things. "How can there be a God of love if He allows this? How can you Christians believe in your God of love? Why would a God of love let my mother die or my wife die? If You are a God of love, why would You do this?" How do we understand it? How do we put all that together?

I don't think I can overstate the importance of answering the questions correctly. All we have to do is look

✝

at how some non-Christians in the world have responded to this sort of thing. You've probably heard of Ted Turner. A man of great wealth and a bitter heart, he is leaving a powerful legacy in the atheistic media. It's easy to view him as an enemy of sorts, but let me give you something to think about. Consider this quote from an interview he had with the *New York Times*:

> Turner is a strident nonbeliever having lost his faith after his sister Mary Jane died of a painful disease. "I was taught that God was love and God was powerful," Turner said, "I couldn't understand how someone so innocent should be made or allowed to suffer so."[1]

Turner is not an isolated case. Some of the most atheistic, humanistic, ardent opponents of our creation ministry claim they were brought up in Bible-believing churches — and yet heart-wrenching circumstances caused them to walk away from their faith. You know what I believe has happened? Many were brought up in churches where Christianity was imposed upon them but they weren't taught how to defend the Christian faith. They never learned to interpret circumstances with the truth of the Word. Instead, they grew up interpreting the Bible according to circumstance. When they faced the tension regarding the difficult questions about evil and suffering, the circumstances led them to believe that God either didn't exist or that He was uncaring or passive.

Significantly, we see this again in the life of Charles Darwin. Darwin grew up going to church and his family continued to do so after he married. But Darwin had a daughter named Annie, and when she became ill, Charles' life was deeply impacted. It is said in his biography that:

> Any vestige of belief in God left him when his daughter Annie died. Annie's cruel death destroyed Charles' tatters and belief in a moral and just universe. Later he would say that this period claimed the final death nail for his Christianity. Charles now took his stand as an unbeliever.[2]

A couple of years ago, PBS did a series on evolution. In one of the programs they portrayed the progression of Darwin's life after his daughter Annie died. At one point they show him going to church with his family. But once they get there, Charles waits outside as his family goes into worship . . . he's unwilling to play a hypocrite and go through the motions of religion as his faith continues to flounder. While the family is in church and Darwin ponders the fate of his daughter, the singing of a hymn filters out of the church. Do you know the hymn they had them singing? "All Thing Bright and Beautiful, the Lord God Made Them All." You know what PBS was trying to say here, don't you. Here is Charles suffering over the death of his daughter Annie and everyone in the church is singing "All Things Bright and Beautiful, The Lord God Made Them All." It's the same irony we found in the movie *Madagascar*, except in Darwin's case, the loss of his daughter was *real*, the tears he shed were *real* . . . and the questions he wrestled with deep in his soul were *real*. Finding no suitable answers to the issues that tormented his soul, he turned his back on the church, abandoned his childhood beliefs, and set out to explain the origin of life without "god."

It's easy to point the finger at non-Christians who have struggled with "the question." But the Christian response hasn't been much better. Many tend to ignore the issue altogether; some just hide the doubt under the surface of their faith while others cloak the problem under a covering of spiritual-sounding clichés.

I think one of the reasons that many people — and many young people — in our churches struggle with their faith is because the teaching and music give the message that the Christian life is supposed to be carefree and problem free. We teach children songs that say "I'm happy all the time. Since Jesus Christ came in, and saved my soul from sin . . . I'm happy all the time." Meanwhile, they are getting beat up on the playground, watching the latest flooding on the 5:00 news, and listening to their parents fight in the evening. Nowhere does Scripture promise a "happy" life, and we should not insinuate otherwise. Again, we point at nature and try to tell them it's all good and beautiful, but in reality, it is *literally* a "dog-eat-dog world," full of anger and death . . . and the Christian is not exempt.

While some struggle, some just deny reality. Even though we all see people dying around us every day, many of us have, at some level of our consciousness, convinced ourselves that this will not happen to us. In a way, we try to avoid reality in order to somehow think that we can get out of dealing with death. But when someone close to us dies, or there is a major tragedy like the destruction of the World Trade Center in New York in 2001, we don't know how to deal with it. We sorrow for a while, but soon we shelve the issue again and get on with life.

In the long run, it doesn't help to deny. The issues will re-surface in some way, at some time. Those who are most honest, yet have the fewest answers, seem to be at risk the most . . . and sometimes they lash out in the process. Every day, anger and frustration boils over in our youth, sometimes with deadly force. A young man who shot and killed his parents and two fellow high school students in Springfield, Oregon, wrote these words:

> It is easier to hate than love because there is so much more hate and misery in the world than there is love and peace. Look at our history — it's full of death, depression, rape, wars, and diseases.[3]

Are you beginning to see that "the question" is a big issue out there? *How can there be a God of love? Look at all the hate. Look at all the awful things in the world. A loving, caring God must not exist.* As Christians, if we are going to be consistent, we have to be able to explain a world where we have joy and we have sorrow, a world where we have both life and death, both love and hate . . . all at the same time. How do we do that? Reality seems so incompatible with the concept of a God of love. How *do* we explain it?

QUESTIONS FOR GROUP DISCUSSION:

1. If someone came to your church and asked the question "If God is love, why is there suffering and death?" what might the average member say? How would your pastor respond?

2. Do you agree that it is not accurate to use "the beauty in nature" as an example of God's love and creativity? Why or why not? How do you think nature should be used for evangelism?

3. Do you know of other people who, like Ted Turner and Charles Darwin, abandoned their faith in God after the devastating death of a loved one? What other tragic circumstances might cause someone to question God?

QUESTIONS FOR PERSONAL REFLECTION:

1. If someone asked you why bad things happen to good people, what would you say?

2. In what ways has the Christian life not lived up to your expectations? What specific circumstances cause you to doubt God's goodness or power?

3. Do you have a good answer to "the question"? If you don't, how might that affect your faith in the future? How might your life be different if you had a clear and concise answer to this important question?

BIBLE VERSES FOR CONTEMPLATION AND MEMORIZATION:

Genesis 1

Romans 1:20

John 16:33

Endnotes
1. "Turner Was Suicidal After Breakup," NYTimes.com, April 16, 2001.
2. Adrian Desmond and James Moore, *Darwin: The Life of a Tormented Evolutionist* (New York: W.W. Norton & Company, 1991), p. 387.
3. Kip Kinkle, excerpts from "Love Sucks," www.pbs.org.

CHAPTER TWO

Only "Time and Death"?

A question as important and as integrated as the one dealing with pain, suffering, and death cannot be answered superficially. Too many people offer answers with little substance and even less supporting evidence. In order to sufficiently address these critical issues of our existence, we *must* go in depth, digging deep into our most essential foundations of belief. That foundation of personal belief is often called a "world view." It

39

is made up of your most basic perceptions about reality and truth. From your world view emerge your interpretations of everything that you see, and it is the core of every decision you make.

As we now address the question *If God is a good and loving God, why is there pain and suffering in the world?* it is absolutely essential that we first investigate the two main world views upon which people have built their answers. You'll soon see that these two world views are diametrically opposed to each other — and as you face difficult circumstances, these two world views will go to war with each other on the battlefield of your heart.

Man's View: Time and Death

The secular-humanist world view (sometimes called "man's view") begins with the assumption that physical matter is the only thing that exists. According to this view, everything that exists was created at "the big bang," where all the matter of the universe appeared in a violent explosion out of nothing. (No one claims to know what *caused* this explosion, but they do claim that it happened and that's where time and space began.) Somehow, the matter that came from nowhere spontaneously arranged itself (with no outside influence or organization) into the first complex living cells over the course of billions of years and the random interaction of chemicals and molecules. Then, over the next hundreds of millions of years, these simple cells are believed to have "evolved" by natural processes into the forms we see today. That process of evolution supposedly took place through chance genetic mutations and a process called "natural selection" in which only the fittest of organisms survive long enough to reproduce. (We will not take the time to dispute this idea in depth in this book. For a detailed bibliography of titles that disprove evolution from many angles, please consult the resource section at the end of this book.)

The late Dr. Carl Sagan said, "The secrets of evolution are time and death."[1] He believed that the process of death and bloodshed, over millions of years, had the result of one kind of organism changing into another, with one kind of animal changing into another, and eventually humans evolving from primates.

In order to try to categorize life and explain how evolution has progressed, secular scientists have attempted to create a "phylogenetic tree" that traces the history of life. In reality this is a "tree of death" because it is based on natural selection (where the weaker organisms are killed), passing on to the next generation only the supposed benefits of genetic mutation. (In the *vast* majority of cases, however, genetic mutations weaken, rather than strengthen an organism . . . a fact that makes this theory mathematically impossible.)

Those who cling to the theory of evolution often appeal to circumstantial scientific "evidence" to prove their point — but I find time and time again that they are not motivated by the evidence at all. A proper interpretation of the same evidences (including an awareness of the most foundational laws of physics) leads one to conclude that matter and life *must* have been *caused* by an outside influence that both designed and created it. That "outside influence" implies that there is a God, and what I observe is that many evolutionists object to the idea of God on moral or philosophical grounds *first*, and then attempt to disprove "God" with science.

The moral/philosophical objection is often stated as the question "If God is all-powerful and loving, why do we see children dying, people suffering, and bad things happening to good people?" Surely such suffering and evil means that either He is not powerful or good, or that He doesn't exist at all. If there's a God of love and you say He is a merciful God and the Bible says God alone is infinite, why does He let all this death and suffering go on? Is He not powerful enough to overcome it? Surely an all-powerful God could stop all this death, destruction, and decay."

Many people have asked these questions with sincerity. Many have not been able to answer them sufficiently, and have rejected the "idea of god," turning to the secular-humanist world view based on evolutionary theory as their new foundation for life. In response to painful and difficult circumstance (often the untimely or painful death of a loved one, or an unjust personal abuse suffered) they begin to interpret everything in a way that attempts to disprove God's existence. While our debates with the evolutionists tend to focus on science and evidence, this is not always the true objection they have against God. Their arguments are usually fueled with passion and pain. Many lash out in great agony over a great loss or "injustice" in their personal lives; many feel neglected or abandoned by people, the Church, or God himself . . . and I can relate. I have been there with the likes of Charles Darwin and Ted Turner. I, too, have had to face the questions.

My Brother

I loved my brother Robert. As an earthly brother and also as my brother-in-Christ, we had much in common, sharing the most important things life has to offer, the things that bond you together on a soul level. Both of us were in Christian work, teaching the Word of God. Over the years, we spent countless hours on the phone and in person discussing personal issues. We had grown together both physically and spiritually as children. Now as adults and fathers we continued to sharpen each other in our faith and in our family.

My wife Mally was the first to begin to notice that something was changing over time — not changing in Robert, but in me. I was getting irritated. My regular telephone conversations with Rob were becoming a source of frustration and Mally picked up on this. "I don't understand," I would often say. "He is becoming so difficult to deal with." Our theological conversations began to degenerate into disjointed arguments and it began to make me feel defensive and angry.

Others in the family began to notice something as well. Most concluded that Robert (like many pastors) was suffering from great stress resulting from his position and ministry. One day I received a very disturbing phone call from one of my best friends. He faithfully attended Rob's church — even though he lived over an hour away — because he loved Rob's verse-by-verse Bible teaching. On this particular day, he had taken some of his visiting relatives to the church, but was greatly disturbed because the sermon Rob gave seemed to lack logic and was very disjointed. He told me that the sermon basically didn't make sense.

Many in his congregation shared these feelings and some were beginning to take offence at his changing demeanor. Our phone conversations began to focus on the people who were leaving the church. Time after time Rob would tell me that another family had left. I couldn't understand what was happening. Those around him kept saying he was suffering from severe stress. That seemed to be a possible explanation, so eventually friends and family convinced Rob to take a break from the ministry and encouraged him to rest and recuperate.

But rest and recuperation never came. He wasn't getting better. We all realized something serious was wrong, but none of us were prepared for what was revealed after a barrage of tests over many months. At age 43, Rob was diagnosed with a degenerative brain disease for which there was no earthly cure. He would never again preach the Word of God as he had so loved to do.

On one level, the diagnosis made complete sense, solving a physical riddle that had perplexed us for quite some time. We finally knew what the problem was. But on another level, the diagnosis hit us like a tornado, causing our thoughts and our faith to be thrown about in a swirling, confusing cloud. Sure, we now knew *what* the problem was . . . but now we had to face the question of *why*.

Why? Why would a loving and all-powerful God allow a dedicated man of God to be struck down in the prime of life? Why should he be subject to such a dreadful, dehumanizing disease — one that caused him to lose his mental faculties, his muscular function, his dignity? Why should his wife and young sons be forced to endure this, watching helplessly in agony of their own as their husband and father degenerated toward a certain and painful death?

"But he was such a great preacher; he stood firmly on the Word of God; he preached the gospel; he wouldn't knowingly compromise God's Word," said my mother.

"I still don't understand why God would allow this to happen to him!"

My breaking point was reached one day when I took Rob to a local shopping center. I thought this would be a simple outing, but it turned out to be one of those heart-gripping, emotional events that I'll never forget . . . one that has been indelibly impressed on my mind. By this time, the disease had taken quite a hold and he couldn't speak much. He was difficult to control and wanted to wander off and grab things out of the stores. Just dealing with this, and watching a man who had been so upright in character do things we had to apologize for, was gut-wrenching. (That day I realized I was only experiencing an infinitesimally small amount of what his wife and children had to put up with. What were they feeling, having to deal with this day after day, concerning their husband and father? Only those who have lived through such a horrific ordeal could even begin to understand what they must have gone through.)

At the shopping center, Rob sat down with me to eat one of his favorite meals — Aussie meat pie and "mushy" peas. Suddenly, Rob saw some people in Muslim garb walking by. He jumped up and ran to them. "Wrong, wrong!" he shouted out. I gripped the table and held back my tears. Rob stared at the Muslims; they stopped and looked perplexed. "Wrong! Wrong!" he continued to say. Somewhere deep inside, Rob's soul still carried that burden to tell Muslims the truth about God — in his heart still burned the passion to see them come to know the forgiveness of Christ and be set free from the slavery of their religion. The passion for others and for God's Word that had directed his life was still intact, still driving him from within, but his brain could no longer communicate the message of the gospel that had been the focus of his preaching. "Wrong! Wrong!" was all he continued to shout. I ran to Rob, held him close, and apologetically led him away from the stunned Muslims and the gathering crowd.

That's when "the question" became vividly real to me. *Why, why, God? Why Robert? Why this way?*

Back at the table, I did my best to regain some composure. Meat pie and mushy peas, a spoon at a time. . . . Across from me sat my brother, a hollow shell of his former self. *Why?*

As I began to search for answers, my mind went back to our childhood. I saw vivid memories of the good times when we played together, those special days when our parents took us camping, the laughter and normal jostling that takes place between siblings. One doesn't usually think about death at that time of one's life. Even growing up as a teenager I had to attend a funeral or two, but it still didn't really hit me that this could happen to me or someone very close to me. The older I get, the more I have to deal with the death of people, of course.

The issue of death and separation from a loved one or special friend really begins to hit home. The first time I had to face such a thing was when my father died . . . but my father died at what most would consider to be an "appropriate" age. Now I was facing the death of my brother, someone in the prime of life, someone younger in age than myself.

How was I to answer? Like Darwin and Turner, my faith in God stood at a crossroad. It felt precarious and uncertain. But thankfully, during that critical season, I had something that many, many people don't: I had a heritage. I had been born and raised in a family that used God's Word as its final authority in all things. I had been taught and discipled in churches that taught the Bible as truth, trusting in its timeless wisdom. Through the example of my father and my experiences in the ministry of Answers in Genesis, I had also learned to think critically, to dissect and defend attacks against God and the Word.

Responding to the Objection

I need you to do a little thinking with me for a moment, for the problem of evil and suffering isn't just a personal one, it's also a *philosophical* one. The question is not only one of science, theology, and/or emotion. It's also a question of logic, so we will first respond with logic. The basic argument against the existence of God based on evil and suffering sounds like this:

A good God would not allow or cause bad things to happen.

Bad things happen.

Therefore, God must not exist.

In order for this argument to have meaning, we must first consider the meaning of "good." Matthew 19:16–17 addresses this very question:

> And behold, one came to Him and said, "Teacher, what good thing shall I do that I may obtain eternal life?" And He said to him, "Why are you asking Me about what is good? There is only One who is good. . . ."

In this passage, Jesus was challenging the man to realize the implications of what he had asked. Jesus pointed out that *only an infinite being who is infinitely good should be called "good."* Jesus' point is that God *is* good, and goodness is defined *by* Him.

I want you to think about this: Only the person who believes in God has a basis to make moral judgments to determine what is "good" and what is "bad." Those who claim that God does not exist have absolutely no authority upon which to call something right or wrong. If God doesn't exist, who can objectively define what is good and what is bad? What basis could there be to make

✠

such judgments? The atheist has no basis upon which to call anything good or bad. They can talk about good and bad, and right and wrong — but it's all relative, it's all arbitrary. What's "good" in one person's mind might be completely "bad" in another's.

So here is the point: In order for "good" and "bad" to exist, God must exist. The unbeliever does not, of course, accept that there is such a being. That means that when he makes the claim that a "good" God and "bad" things in this world cannot be reconciled, he cannot make the claim without assuming that God, indeed, does exist. If he doesn't, his argument falls apart!

In other words, the atheist has a big problem when he argues against God on the basis of "good" and "bad." Because in order for "good" and "bad" to exist, God *must* exist. The assumption that "good" and "bad" exist *assumes* that there is a God. Anyone who speaks of "good" and "bad" has to presuppose a world view that includes God, because without a godly world view there can be no absolute authority to define those words.

Christian apologist Greg Bahnsen stated it this way:

> Philosophically speaking, the problem of evil turns out to be, therefore, a problem for the unbeliever himself. In order to use the argument from evil against the Christian world view, he must first be able to show that his judgments about the existence

of evil are meaningful, which is precisely what his unbelieving world view is unable to do.[2]

The bottom line is this: Arguments involving "good," "bad," "right," "wrong," etc. cannot be used to disprove the existence of God. Philosophically, they actually show that God *does* exist. This doesn't reconcile the problem of a good God co-existing with an evil world, but it does demolish the faulty logic that some use to dismiss God altogether.

Actually, there is no good answer to the question that asks "How could a good God exist when there is so much bad in the world?" *There is no good answer because it's a bad question to begin with!* It's called a "self-defeating" argument. There is a much better question that must be addressed — and we will do so shortly. But first, let's consider the tragic consequences of dismissing God on these grounds.

Meaninglessness

The secular-humanist world view has no answer to the questions concerning the problems from evil and suffering. In fact, it has no answer to much of anything. In a world without God, everything must have happened just by chance and random processes. There was no intent, no design, no purpose . . . it all "just happened." In such a world, there is no true meaning to anything. Life is tough, and then you die. Period.

✝

Dr. Richard Dawkins is an atheist and one of the world's leading spokespersons for evolution. An interviewer once made this statement to him: "The idea of evolution and natural selection makes some people feel that everything is meaningless, people's individual lives and life in general." Dr. Dawkins responded that, "If it's true that it causes people to feel despair. That's tough. If it's true, its true; and you had better live with it."[3] So if I believe in atheistic evolution and it causes me to despair, what can I do? *Be tough. Get used to it. That's what it's all about. Live with it.*

And then he was asked this question, "What do you see is the problem with a terminally ill cancer patient believing in an afterlife?" Dr. Dawkins responded, "No problem at all. If I could have word with a would-be suicide bomber who thinks he is going to paradise, I would say 'Don't imagine for one second that you are going to paradise, you're going to rot in the ground.' " At least Dr. Dawkins is consistent and honest. Without God, nothing matters. *It doesn't matter if you are terminally ill or if you are a terrorist. You are going to die, and that is the end of it. Life, then, is utterly meaningless. Nothing you can do will make a difference. When you die, you won't even remember you were here, and in a short time, no one else will remember you either. Life has no meaning; it never did; it doesn't now; and it never will. It's just time and death. That's all. That's tough. Get used to it.*

By the way, if what Dr. Dawkins is saying is true, why does he bother arguing about anything? What's the point? Think about it! I have often wondered why an atheistic evolutionist would bother trying to convince someone of something. They believe that when you die that's the end of you. Isaac Asimov believed that, Carl Sagan believed that, and that's what Richard Dawkins is saying. *When you die, you rot, that's it.* From that perspective, you won't even know you were ever here; you won't even know you ever existed. You won't remember any of it . . . and neither will anyone else; so therefore, what is the point of arguing with the creationists? I don't understand the point.

I remember a guy who came up to me after one of my talks at the University in Dublin in Ireland. He was fairly upset by the things I had taught and said, "When you are dead, you're dead! You prove to me there's life after death! When you're dead, you're dead!"

I thought, *Well, I can't prove scientifically that there's life after death; true science just can't prove such things.* So I started to talk to him about some of the things I said in the lecture and what the Bible said. But he just kept saying, "When you're dead, you're dead. When you're dead, you're dead. When you're dead, you're dead!"

So finally, I got so frustrated I said, "Well, if that's it, *when you're dead, you're dead,* you won't even know you existed, won't even know you're alive, won't even remember this conversation . . . you won't even know you were here. You won't know *anything* so it's as if you never existed!" And then I told him "You may as well go and jump off a cliff right now!" And he said, "You know what, I may as well, just to show you!" And I thought, "Uh oh. Now I've done it. This bloke is going to do himself in because of my lecture!" Well, we both settled down a little and talked a little more. And you know what? He actually came back to the seminar the next night and asked me for a book about God.

It's an odd situation, when you think about it. The Bible says that everyone knows in their heart that God exists and yet so many try in futility to "disprove" Him. Romans 1:20 says:

> For since the creation of the world His invisible attributes, His eternal power and divine nature, have been clearly seen, being understood through what has been made, so that they are without excuse.

So the atheist claims that because of "bad" things, a "good" God cannot exist . . . but in the process, he actually has to assume that God does exist. The evolutionist claims that life has no meaning and that there is no "truth," and yet many of them have devoted their lives to convincing others that their point of view is true. The man in Dublin claimed that "when you're dead, you're dead," yet he came back again with the hope that maybe there would be life after all.

So again, let me assure you that the secular-humanist world view has no answer for the problems of suffering and death . . . and in times of trouble, they not only face complete meaninglessness in the circumstances, but they also have nowhere to look (other than themselves) for strength. I must say, I often wonder how a non-Christian can even begin to cope in situations like the one our family had found itself in. For such a person, this life, as far as they believe, is all there is. When a loved one dies, they believe that is the end of them — they exist no more. How they must despair. But surely, it must even be more despairing to think that *if this life is all there is, then even the few years we have are utterly meaningless.* No wonder Paul says in 1 Thessalonians 4:13, "Brothers, we do not want you to be ignorant about those who fall asleep, or to grieve like the rest of men, who have no hope" (NIV).

The Right Question

I hope that you are beginning to realize that a deep question cannot be resolved with a superficial answer. It should be clear by now that the world view that lies at the foundation of our thinking will ultimately determine the course of our thoughts. As we look at the secular-humanist world view, we see that not only is it based on a faulty interpretation of scientific fact, but its atheistic conclusions are based on faulty logic . . . logic that leads to a meaningless, futile existence. Because non-Christians have been indoctrinated to believe that our existence is the result of nothing more than *time and death* (millions of years of suffering, disease, bloodshed, and death), they are not going to understand about a God of love until they begin to see life through a true, uncompromised Christian world view that includes the correct time-line of history.

So at this point, we can see what the wrong question is . . . but we have yet to find an answer as well, for the secular world view has none to offer. As Bible-believing Christians, however, we begin with a totally different set of assumptions. We *begin* with the fact that a good God *does* exist. Through the witness of the inerrant Scriptures, a right interpretation of scientific fact, and the understandings that God has placed in our hearts, we can presuppose a Christian world view that says *God is there.*

From there we can now ask the *right* question: How do you explain death and suffering in a world where an all-powerful, loving, and just God exists? That's the question believers wrestle with, isn't it? We know that God *is*, and we know that He is *good*. Desperately, we seek reconciliation between the pain and evil we see and this loving God we believe in.

Thankfully, when we turn to the Bible for answers and let His Word speak for itself, that reconciliation takes place both in the mind and in the heart.

QUESTIONS FOR GROUP DISCUSSION:

1. Describe in your own words the secular-humanist belief in "time and death." If you had to debate in favor of this view, what evidence might you use? How would you defend yourself against this view?

2. On philosophical grounds, we can dismiss the question "How could a good God exist when there is so much bad in the world?" Do you think that is appropriate? How might someone who feels wounded by God respond to this dismissal?

3. Do you think secular-humanism always leads to fatalism? Why or why not?

QUESTIONS FOR PERSONAL REFLECTION:

1. In what ways has the idea of evolution influenced your thinking?

2. From a scientific/historical perspective, what questions do you have pertaining to creation?

3. Spend a few moments looking through the resource section at the end of this book, then go to www. AnswersInGenesis.org. Are there any questions that you have that couldn't be answered with resources like these?

BIBLE VERSES FOR CONTEMPLATION AND MEMORIZATION:

James 1:2–5

Romans 1:20–22

Endnotes
1. Carl Sagan, "Cosmos, Episode #2: One Voice in the Cosmic Fugue," Public Broadcasting Service, 1980.
2. G.L. Bahnsen, *Always Ready — Directions for Defending the Faith* (Nacogdoches, TX: Covenant Media Press, 2002), p. 169.
3. Laura Sheahen, "The Problem with God: Interview with Richard Dawkins," interview conducted at the World Congress of Secular Humanism, October 2005, www.Beliefnet.com.

CHAPTER THREE

The Big Picture

Throughout Europe, many of the great cathedrals and castles of the world still stand tall today, marking an era of human history and creativity unique and unmatched: the Renaissance. Some of these magnificent structures date to medieval times, just before the Renaissance. While decorated with gold and elaborate tapestry, among the most impressive elements of their construction are the artistic images that often begin underfoot, span the walls, and then arch across the ceilings. From a distance, they flow seamlessly from scene to scene, displaying in glowing detail the stories and likenesses that the artist sought to record. From up close, however, an unbelievable reality emerges: these massive works of art are actually mosaics; consisting of millions — *hundreds of millions* — of minute, single-colored tiles, each placed one-by-one over the course of decades. The closer you are, the more the tiles themselves dominate your vision . . . and the harder it is to see how the pieces fit into the larger work. When you are very close, you can't tell at all what you are looking at . . . the tiles look like a random and senseless assortment of pieces.

That's where I found myself in the winter of 2000. As I struggled to answer the questions about what was happening to my brother, I found that I was too close to the situation to see clearly; my heart was too near the pain to make sense of what was going on. That's when I knew I needed to stand back and begin to look at what was happening from a bit of a distance. In the midst of the difficult details of what we were facing, I needed to put things in the context of the "big picture."

For years, I've been committed to the "big picture." Starting with the Word of God, its history, and its principles, I've always sought to build a world view based on Scripture. It's a framework of sorts; a grid of truth that can then be used to analyze the specific situations and the "evidence" we see around us. In that way, I've always tried to present a broad, biblical view in regard to issues that really affect our culture. Just like a mosaic, viewing the larger perspective allows us to see the details for what they are, and they then find meaning in the sum of the whole picture.

The true biblical "big picture" encompasses a Christian world view that begins with Creation, then proceeds to Corruption, Catastrophe, Confusion, Christ, Cross, and Consummation. An understanding of the entirety of human history — the past as well as what is prophesied for the future — allows us to properly place ourselves within it, seeing more clearly what might appear to be random, unexplained events.

At this point, it's important that you know that simply because you are a Christian, doesn't mean that you have a Christian world view. In fact, very few Christians see the world correctly. Many of us have been indoctrinated to believe in some sort of mixture of the secular-humanist world view and the biblical one. Even though they might believe in Christ as their Savior, they might also believe in Darwinian evolution and that there were millions of years of suffering and death in nature before man evolved. Even though they believe in a God of love, they can't respond adequately to the questions of the non-Christian. When difficult times come, a Christian who adheres to the worldly perspective of human history and origins suffers from confusion over reality, finding themselves without an awareness of the "big picture" that might help them make sense out of the detail.

No wonder Christianity seems to have lost its power! Christians have lost biblical Christianity, which is based on the Word of the living God. It's only when the Christian understands the biblical origin of death and suffering that they will be able to give an answer to both the non-Christian and to themselves.

Developing a Christian world view is important . . . and it is a process, as Paul points out in Romans 12:2:

> And do not be conformed to this world, but
> be transformed by the renewing of your mind,
> that you might prove what the will of God is, that
> which is good and acceptable and perfect.

Nowhere is this more important than in dealing with this seemingly perplexing and often painful question regarding the cause of suffering and death. Scripture has the answer to this problem . . . and it's an answer that silences the skeptic and gives comfort and perspective to the perplexed and hurting Christian. But to find it, one must be willing to accept what the Bible says, and often cut through much religious and worldly heresy that has infiltrated the Church. Without a correct time-line, little of this makes sense.

The Big Picture

Before time and space as we experience it, there was God. He is an all-powerful God (Jeremiah 32:17, 27), an eternal God without beginning or end (1 Kings 8:27; Isaiah 57:15), and a God who knows all (Isaiah 48:3–5; 1 John 3:20). He's a merciful and gracious God. Scripture even says that the mercy of the Lord is from everlasting to everlasting (James 5:11; 1 Peter 1:3). He is also a God that loves (John 3:16) and actually *is* love (1 John 4:7–8).

When God created reality as we know it, He did so in six days, and when He was done, He said that everything was very good. In fact, if you look up this word in the original Hebrew, the translation should really be that it was *"exceedingly good."*

It's appropriate to dwell on that for a moment. What He originally made *exceeded* good. I believe it was so good that we really can't imagine what it was like at all! Can you imagine a world that was perfect? Functioning in absolute harmony? Where man and woman walked in complete intimacy with their Creator?

I can't imagine that kind of goodness; yet our earth was such a world. Even among the animal kingdom, death was an unknown. Originally, the animals were vegetarian and man was vegetarian as well. Yes, plants were eaten, and as Dr. Hugh Ross notes,[1] they "suffered" in this way, yet they clearly lack a brain to interpret this as pain. Scripture itself makes an important distinction between plants and animals at this point. In Genesis 1, we see a general Hebrew term — *nephesh*. This word refers to living creatures such as man and animals. The word doesn't apply to plants, but it does apply to vertebrates. The Bible clearly distinguishes between animals that have a *nephesh* and the plants and insects which do not. So the Bible would not classify plants as living creatures in the same way as those that have blood and flesh.

The death of creatures with *nephesh* carries a different weight, even to us as humans. If you are out in the mountains and see the form of a large sun-bleached tree stump, twisted and weathered, you might look at this dead tree and think *Wow, that is beautiful.* We even decorate our homes with dead and dried plants. But what would the neighbors think if you decorated with the dead carcass of a dog or something? Or if you were in the woods and saw the decayed remains of an elk, would you think *Wow, nice. Let's stop here for the picnic!* No, there's something different about animal death, isn't there?

Originally, there was no death for those who had *nephesh.* In Genesis 1:29–30 we read:

> I have given you every plant . . . and it shall
> be food for you; and to every beast of the earth
> and to every bird of the sky and to everything that

moves on the earth which has life, I have given every green plant for food.

Even though only plants were eaten as part of God's original creation, it wasn't until Genesis 9:3 — after the Flood — that God said, "Every moving thing that is alive shall be food for you; I give all to you. . . ." Somewhere between these two mandates a change occurred, but that's not the way it started. Originally, it was a *beautiful* world. It was *exceedingly* good. Pain, suffering, and death did not exist, and Adam and Eve walked freely with their God, uncovered and not ashamed in any way.

But then, it became corrupted, all of it. What happened? How did we get to the place we are at today? In Genesis, we again find the historical account of the actions that have led to our present realities.

The Choice

The LORD God commanded the man, saying, "From any tree of the garden you may eat freely; but from the tree of the knowledge of good and evil you shall not eat, for in the day that you eat from it *you will surely die*" (Genesis 2:16–17).

The command was clear and the implications were obvious. A line had been drawn and mankind was instructed to obey and live. But soon enough, Satan, the father of lies, would twist the command with a subtle

✝

deceit, with a half-truth that would cause Eve to question the intent of the command, appealing to the same desire we each face every day:

> The serpent said to the woman, "You surely shall not die! For God knows that in the day you eat from it your eyes will be opened, *and you will be like God,* knowing good and evil" (Genesis 3:4–5).

At that pivotal moment in history a choice was made that altered the course of humanity, sending shock waves forever into the future; spreading lies, pain, isolation, and death to all generations.

> . . . she took from its fruit and ate; and she gave also to her husband with her, and he ate.

The implications of their disobedience were immediate and obvious: A sense of guilt and nakedness overcame them, and they hid from the One who had made them. Phillip Yancey described it this way:

> By their choice they put distance between themselves and God. Before, they had walked and talked with God. Now when they heard his approach, they hid in the shrubbery. An awkward separation had crept in to spoil the intimacy.

And every quiver of disappointment in our own relationship with God is an aftershock from their initial act of rebellion.[2]

Next came the blame game. When God confronted them, Adam pointed the finger at Eve and Eve pointed to the serpent, each attempting to dodge the responsibility for what they had done. But it was too late, the damage had been done. Forever, humanity would be born into a cursed and broken world; one filled with pain and hardship — and at the end of it all we face the certainty of death:

> By the sweat of your face you shall eat bread, till you return to the ground, because from it you were taken; for you are dust, and to dust you shall return (Genesis 3:19).

Throughout Scripture, the Bible points to this event — "the fall" of man — as the origin of death. In Romans 5:12, for example, Paul states, "Therefore, just as through one man sin entered into the world, and death through sin, and so death spread to all men, because all sinned." Later, in 6:23 he asserts that "the wages of sin is death," and in 1 Corinthians 15:56 we read, "The sting of death is sin."

Here we see one of the great contrasts between the secular-humanist world view, which claims that reality has been directed by "*time* and death," and the biblical world view that shows life in this fallen world is accounted for by *sin* and death.

Not only does sin account for the separation we experience with God and the origin of death, but it also accounts for the decay and destruction we see in nature. Romans 8:22 tells us that "the whole creation groans and suffers the pains. . . ."

For example, when we look at something like the tsunami, we could rightly call it a *sin*ami, because it is a natural consequence of Adam's disobedience. When Adam sinned, it sent shock waves through the entire universe, including nature. The covenant relationship between Adam and God was broken, as was the covenant relationship between Adam and the creation! In the beginning, God had placed man in dominion over creation, giving us the authority to subdue it. But now, the creation is in rebellion against man, often with deadly consequences.

Please understand the implications of this: It's not God's fault there's death in the world. *It's our fault.* And just like Adam, we would much rather point to someone else, or something else, rather than take responsibility for it ourselves. There is a remnant of beauty and a shadow of goodness on this planet, but when we look at all the horrible things going on, we don't want to admit that we are the ones who are to blame. We want to accuse somebody else. We want to blame God, or the politicians, or our parents . . . always pointing elsewhere, rather than face the fact that we are dead in our own trespasses and sin.

Jeremiah 17:9 says that "the heart of man is deceitful above all things, and desperately wicked" (NKJV). But instead of us saying, "Look what *our* sin did to the world!" You know what we want to say? "Why does *God* do that?" We don't want to admit the horrible thing that we did (and continue to do) when we sin. When we disobey, we are truly committing high treason against the God of creation. Do you realize how bad that sin is? Just look at what it has done to the world! Rather than shaking our fists at the heavens, we should be falling down on our knees in prayer saying, as Paul did, "Wretched man that I am! Who will set me free from the body of this death?" (Romans 7:24).

No, it's not God's fault — responsibility lies with each of us and with all of us. Isaiah 59:1–2 restates the corruptive and divisive implications of sin in different words:

> Behold, the LORD's hand is not so short that it cannot save; neither is His ear so dull that it cannot hear. But your iniquities have made a separation between you and your God, and your sins have hidden His face from you, so that He does not hear.

And it all started that one day in Eden when Adam and Eve succumbed to the temptation to become like God. The rest is history, and because we are all descendents of Adam, his history is our heritage. In numerous places the Bible refers to us being "in Adam." When Adam sinned, we were all "in" Adam, and thus must suffer the consequences of his rebellious action against a Holy God. (And of course we have all individually taken part in that rebellion in our own lives, too.) So since that day, we have been given a death sentence at the point of conception . . . and like Adam, we are naturally inclined to deny it and try to shift the blame.

As the days passed and Robert's body and mind continued a slow and steady destruction at the hands of his disease, this "big picture" presented in Scripture began to give me a perspective from which I could make sense of the suffering Robert was facing and the death that was at hand. Now, both the question and the answer were becoming very clear.

How do you explain death and suffering in a world where an all-powerful, loving, and just God exists? You explain it with sin; Adam's sin and our personal sin.

For many, however, the truth about sin and death (and our personal responsibility for it) is not an acceptable answer. Yes, it's hard to face the truth sometimes, and many who don't want to face the message will try to undermine the messenger. In our case, in this contemporary world, that means that many who don't want to take responsibility for sin and its consequences will try to attack the truth at its source . . . that source being the Word of God.

Defending the Source of Truthful Answers

My brother was a devoted defender of the Bible. Robert also understood that the history in Genesis is foundational to the rest of Scripture — and foundational to a correct big picture of life, for all Christian doctrine is founded in the Genesis history. Robert also believed that Genesis makes it plain that there was no death, bloodshed, or disease before sin, and that sin originated at "the Fall" and continues through our personal actions.

Robert so wanted to teach people God's Word, and was continually searching for the best tools to help him do so. A year or so before he was stricken with this terrible disease, Rob excitedly told me about a Bible study program produced by a well-known Australian theological college. However, he was immensely saddened to find that this program compromised the Word of God in the Book of Genesis with evolutionary teaching.

Rob believed that the Bible could not accommodate the notion that life had evolved over millions of years, as this Bible study program did. To do so would be to admit that the Bible's words cannot be trusted and that God is an ogre. Integral to the notion of evolution is the idea that the fossil record — with its evidence of death, disease, suffering, and violence — was laid down millions of years

✝

before man came on the scene. But the Bible says that at the end of the sixth day of creation — after finishing the creation of all living things including Adam and Eve — God described the creation as "very good" (Genesis 1:31). As Rob once said to me during one of our phone calls, "If God said death, suffering, disease, and violence is 'very good,' then God is an ogre. No, God created a perfect creation that has been corrupted by sin. There is no way the billions of fossils could have been laid down before man. I believe you're right in saying that most of the fossils resulted from the flood of Noah's day, not from millions of years of death prior to the sin of man."

He knew that it was the sin of the first man, Adam, which resulted in the judgment of death and the entrance of disease, suffering, and violence into the world. Yet the Genesis section of this Bible study program had adopted the secular world view of time-and-death evolution and this was extremely upsetting to Rob. He saw what this theological college had done as an attack on God's Word — and like our father, Rob hated compromise. He realized that if one could take man's fallible interpretation of the world and reinterpret the Bible accordingly in Genesis, then this could be done with any passage in the Bible. People could start questioning the Resurrection or the virgin birth. And after all, no scientist has seen anyone rise from the dead, so maybe this part of the Bible should be reinterpreted also!

As a devout defender of the Bible, Rob wrote to the president of the college and eventually visited him, challenging him personally concerning this matter. Here is a portion of that letter:

> If death came into this world as a result of Adam's sin, where is there place for the evolutionary process? The evolutionary process is a process of death and struggle. If we were simply guided by the Bible with no other influence, I have no doubt that the only conclusion that could be made would be that death came into the world as a result of sin. . . .
>
> Obviously, we do not have all the answers in respect to the original creation, and certain questions remain as a result of the Fall. However, we must acknowledge that we are looking back at a perfect creation through fallen eyes, and our first and authoritative revelation must come from the words of Scripture.
>
> So many people . . . do not approach the creation doctrine from Scripture first, but allow theories and assumptions from certain fields of science to create a framework of thinking that is then taken to Scripture, instead of the other way around.

✝

When faced with an important issue, Rob would go immediately to the Bible, beginning with Genesis, and answer from there. Without the literal history in Genesis, Rob would not have had a consistent, logical answer; and he would have floundered in poor philosophy and un-ending confusion just as the secular-humanist does when faced with these questions.

But let there be no surprises when the clear answers found in Scripture often cause a stir and are rejected by many. There is no quick-fix solution when it comes to countering more than a century of evolutionary indoctri-nation. Absolute truth is divisive truth, separating dark-ness and light. The humanist knows this is where the real battle is being waged and they will reject us on this point incessantly. Because Christ is the truth, His ministry was divisive as well. He said, "Do not think that I came to bring peace on the earth; I did not come to bring peace, but a sword. For I came to set a man against his father, and a daughter against her mother . . ." (Matthew 10:34–35).

Truthful answers can only come from a truthful source. While many may not receive it, it is only from the source of truth, God's Word, that we can honestly find the foundational answer to the question regarding suffering and death. On the "big picture" foundation we can begin to build a clear understanding of our present circumstances. But without that foundation, what do we have to turn to?

The sincere believer in God, who seeks honest answers to the most perplexing and painful of life's problems, will find that the truth can set you free from the anger, disappointment, and futile hopelessness of the evolutionary world view based on time and death. The biblical world view (encompassing *creation, corruption, catastrophe, confusion, Christ, the cross,* and the *consummation*) gives the necessary perspective we need to face difficult realities.

The "big picture" sure helped me and my family as we wrestled with the questions about what was happening with my brother. How do you explain death and suffering in a world where an all-powerful, loving, and just God exists? The answer is *sin.* While this world had a perfect beginning, it was thrown into death and destruction by the willful choices of Adam and Eve to disobey the Father . . . and we continue to sin day-to-day "in Adam."

As the issues we were facing began to take their place in the biblical world view, I instinctively wanted to reach for the phone and call Rob to discuss these things with him, just as we had for years and years. What would he have to say? How would he apply the Word of God to this situation? As a pastor, how would he have counseled us, and what would he suggest we do in response to the circumstance we were in? I so desired to connect with him one more time. I longed for the opportunity to hear his perspective on what he himself was facing. But of course, as I looked at him now — just an empty shell of the former man he had been — I knew that was impossible . . . *or was it?*

QUESTIONS FOR GROUP DISCUSSION:

1. In your opinion, how would the average person on the street answer the question, "How do you explain death and suffering in a world where an all-powerful, loving, and just God exists?"

2. In regard to the origin of death in nature, Rob once said, "If God said death, suffering, disease, and violence is 'very good,' then God is an ogre. No, God created a perfect creation that has been corrupted by sin. There is no way the billions of fossils could have been laid down before man's sin." Do you agree or disagree with that statement? What reasoning would you give for your answer?

3. If everyone in your family or church accepted the "big picture" world view of God's Word, how would things change?

QUESTIONS FOR PERSONAL REFLECTION:

1. When things go wrong in your life, where do you tend to place the blame? Consider the specific challenges

you face right now. What is the root issue behind these struggles?

2. Read Romans 3:23–24. On a scale of 1 to 10, how would you rate your sinfulness compared to other people? How would you rate yourself according to God's standards of holiness? (See James 2:9–10.)

BIBLE VERSES FOR CONTEMPLATION AND MEMORIZATION:

Isaiah 59:1–2
Romans 5:6–12

Endnotes
1. Hugh Ross, *Creation and Time: A Biblical and Scientific Perspective on the Creation-Date Controversy* (Colorado Springs, CO: Navpress Publishing Group, 1994), p. 63.
2. Philip Yancey, *Disappointment with God* (Grand Rapids, MI: Zondervan, 1992), p. 61–62.

CHAPTER FOUR

A Voice from the Past

Facing a serious illness and the certainty of death is a humbling experience . . . and one that wakes us up by shattering the illusion of security and health that surrounds us in the modern world. If you've walked the halls of a nursing home, you understand what I mean. If you or a loved one has been on the receiving end of a terminal medical diagnosis, you've felt it. If you've been to a funeral or two, you probably know what I'm talking about. In these moments — undistracted by the noise of the world — the reality that what the Bible says is true is seen with unusual clarity . . . and then usually quickly forgotten as one re-enters "regular" life.

As I returned to my room after visiting Rob in the nursing home, my mind was in high gear, still sorting out the implications of his illness. While the "big picture" put "the question" into a biblical framework, many other issues needed to be faced: *What then should one expect out of life? Is this fair? Can God heal, and if so, why doesn't He? How do we help others in situations like ours?*

As the realities of the inevitable loss of my brother intensified, so did my desire to connect with him again. Sure, I could talk *to* him (and did so as I sat at his bed-side) but I was unable to tell if my words were getting through. At this point there was no response at all. How I yearned to hear his voice again; to discuss together what he — and we — were facing. But how could that happen? The very issue had placed a great gap between us, making it impossible for him to reach across the void that his illness had erected between him and the rest of us.

That's when my youngest brother Stephen gave me an audio tape. "You've got to hear this," Stephen said. "It's almost prophetic." The label on the tape read *The Experience Trap. Robert Ham, June 1, 1997.* My mind did the math: This was a sermon that Rob had preached only a couple of years before his major health issue began to manifest itself. "Rob deals directly with the very issue he's being confronted with right now," Steve continued excitedly. "It's like he's giving the sermon to himself!"

I was fairly stunned. What did he have to say that related to this current situation? Did he have some insight I hadn't been given that could throw more light on the situation? Could his words help his family or perhaps encourage others who are grieving over the pain and suffering of a loved one? Could this help us understand how to cope with his present condition? Might the historical and theological reconciliation I sought continue through the concise words of my brother, even as he lay with mumbled speech on his death bed? After looking at the tape for some time, I placed it in the cassette deck and pressed the "play" button. . . .

This morning, I want to address the issues of sin, sickness, and healing from the Word of God. . . .

The health, vigor, and confidence of his words were startling — a complete contrast to who he had become. This was the brother I knew! This was the man whose desire to preach truth could be felt in the urgent intensity of his voice. As his message began to flow, I found myself clinging to every word. It was as if God had been preparing Rob, his family, and his friends for what was coming

✝

— answering ahead of time so many of the specific questions we were now facing.

As the tape rolled on, Rob's words began to speak alongside the Bible's words — the Word which he so deeply trusted and preached — and as they did, the context of the issues we were facing began to find reconciliation not only in my mind, but also in my heart.

Sure, I've taught the "big picture" in reference to geology, the family, and human history, but now, listening to Rob, I wasn't the teacher, I was the student: "You see, if there was no sin in the world . . . there wouldn't be any sickness and there would be no death," he began. "There is not a person in this world who will not die before the Lord Jesus comes again. . . . Death is the ultimate 'sickness' that we all have to face as a result of sin."

When it came to the origin of sin and death, Rob and I were on the same page. We both understood from the Genesis narrative *why* there is suffering. Adam's rebellion in the Garden of Eden had corrupted the original creation and because we are all descendants of Adam and continue to sin, we all suffer the same problem. As he applied the "big picture" to the circumstances we were in — the circumstances *he* was in — many of the questions we were dealing with as he was slowly being destroyed by disease were answered in his own words — even as he now faced certain death.

Isn't This "Abnormal"?

Earlier in the day — the day Steve had given me the tape of Rob's sermon — I had been beside Rob's bed in the nursing home, holding his feeble hand. I kept thinking *This is not normal, Rob. Surely it is not normal for this to happen to such a one as you.* As I looked at his weakened body and his blank and sunken face (that had once been filled with the overflowing joy of his Christian character), I was overcome with the notion that this is not the way it should be, that his condition was not following the expected course of human life.

But that evening, Rob's own words on the tape countered my thoughts . . . it was as if he knew back then what would be on my mind, and he used the example of the apostle Paul to make his point:

> I am going to say this twice. . . . I would like this to melt into your mind and into your heart. I want it to be written indelibly on your mind so that it will never, ever be wiped away. Please understand this. You see the apostle Paul when we look at the whole New Testament. . . . Paul saw illness and he saw sickness as *normal.* Let me spell if for you: N-O-R-M-A-L. I'd like to underline it with a great big felt pen and write it indelibly in every one of our minds. The apostle Paul saw sickness and illness as normal living in a world ruined by

✝

sin. I'll say it again: the apostle Paul saw illness and sickness as normal living in a world that has been ruined by sin.

Rob was right. We should *expect* illness and death. Although sickness is abnormal in the sense that it was not part of the original creation before sin, it should be considered "normal" in this fallen world. Had Rob been with us, helping us deal with his situation (looking on his disease-racked body and knowing the person lying there was a devout Christian) he would say, through tears of compassion, that this is the sort of thing to be expected in a sin-cursed universe. I believe Rob would then tell us that instead of focusing on the disease, we need to focus on Christ.

As Rob continued to develop this part of his sermon on the tape, it became very clear to me what he would say to us now if he were able:

> I know its sad watching my body die and not being able to communicate with me. I know you feel a horrible separation, but look at what the Bible says. It doesn't promise we will be physically healed in this sin-cursed world. Remember, we are all sick and dying because of sin — this is to be considered normal in this world. Even the people who were healed or raised from the dead by Christ during

His earthly ministry or through the Apostles had only a temporary reprieve. Eventually, they had to die anyway. No one can escape this normal course of events for this world. But for the Christian, the wonderful news is that God does promise to comfort us and strengthen us, knowing we are sinful creatures living in such a fallen world.

In Eden, our expectations could have been different. But now, outside the Garden, the consequences of sin dictate our destiny. While our unavoidable confrontations with illness and death will still pierce our hearts with grief, they should not come as a shock. As Peter counseled the first generation of Christians, "Beloved, do not be surprised at the fiery ordeal among you, which comes upon you for your testing, as though some strange thing were happening to you . . ." (1 Peter 4:12).

Yes, illness and death is the norm in this post-Fall era of human history, and we should not expect otherwise.

What about "Original Sin" and Specific Sins?

When trying to discern the root cause of illness, disease, and death, it's not uncommon for us to search out a particular sin that the suffering individual may have committed that has caused the problem. In his message, Rob explained that the consequences of certain sins could lead to sickness. (For example, alcohol abuse can lead to liver damage and unbiblical sexual behavior can lead to AIDS and a host of other very, very serious sexually transmitted diseases.) Also, there are times when God can cause people to become sick because of their rebellion against Him.

Certainly our specific sins can have their consequences in specific illnesses. As Galatians 6:7 says:

> Do not be deceived, God is not mocked; for whatever a man sows, this he will also reap.

But, of course, there are other people who seem to have done nothing to cause their sickness (a baby born HIV positive, for example, or a child with leukemia). And then there are those who die in accidents or disasters that appear to have no direct connection to their personal sin at all. In those situations, the hardship may not be because of any specific sin in their life at all, but because of the sins of others or as a result of the world itself being fallen. Sin has been in the entire world since Adam and Eve rebelled. It is called "original sin," and it affects everyone. Perceived innocence is no insulator against the all-encompassing effects of this sin. Every day bad things happen to good people ("good" as we might compare them to other "bad" people at least, but still sinful by God's standard!). These things come upon us because the world itself is fallen and the consequences of our sins "in Adam" which have been passed down through the generations.

As the tape rolled on, I realized that Robert had not only taught this truth with his words, but he was illustrating it with his own life, before my very eyes, as his mind and body continued their decline.

Isn't This All Very Unfair?

During one of my earlier visits to Australia, before Rob had deteriorated too badly, I took him on a trip to a country town west of Brisbane. He couldn't talk much and when he did, some of his sentences didn't make sense. He kept trying to tell me about his sermons — trying in some way to explain to me his unending love for preaching God's Word. He would say things like, "I did 14 on Genesis, and 10 on Romans and. . . ." I figured that he was telling me about the sermons he had preached on those books but nothing came out right. As he tried to speak he seemed perplexed and his face became as contorted as his words. No matter how hard he tried to explain, he couldn't say it. His memory that was once so full of knowledge concerning God's Word was basically gone. It was such a distressing and pitiful scene.

At this point, Rob could still play the piano and the accordion. We would motion to him to sit down at the piano or get out his accordion, and he would play with a big smile on his face; the music expressing the special talent the Lord had given him. Over time, though, this gift started to disappear. He could play fewer and fewer tunes, until he could play only parts of certain ones. Eventually, all his wonderful abilities in this area ceased.

After the disease had taken considerable control, we still took him to church — knowing that he wouldn't understand (as far as we knew) what was happening. It appeared as if he was still able to read . . . at least he would pick up his favorite books (especially the Bible) and seemingly read the words page after page (although we don't know how much, if anything, he understood). At one of the church services, we stood up to sing a hymn. Though Rob could no longer speak to us, he sang his heart out to the Lord with clear and convincing words. My mother, tears running down her cheeks, watched with breaking heart. But at the end of the service Rob did not seem to know anything about what he had done or what was going on around him.

Intimately involved in all of this of course was Brenda, Rob's wife, and his two sons, Joshua and Geoffrey. Feelings of injustice must have overwhelmed them. Rob did everything because of his love for God and His Word. Now they were watching him die, and it was not just a "normal" death, but a slow, debilitating, and utterly dehumanizing one. How must they have felt as they watched him being robbed of his ability to communicate and play the piano and accordion — the special gifts they all believed God had given him — as his mental faculties left him? How incomprehensible it must have been to see his thoughts and speech, which he had so purposefully developed and used to communicate the gospel, now reduced to nothing.

Sure, it all fit within the biblical framework, but it all seemed so unjust.

During my lifetime, I've heard non-Christians mock God when they see a Christian suffering by saying such things as, "That person doesn't deserve to suffer like that. How can a God of love let someone who serves Him go through such a terrible situation?" Such mockery has made me angry . . . but now we were asking the same questions. Sure, other "bad" people might deserve this kind of a death, but not a God-fearing servant like Rob, right?

I remember the day I received the phone call from his wife, Brenda. We had hoped his brain tests would come back negative; that was when we were still fairly sure that his problems were because of severe stress . . . at least that was our continued hope. However, the tests came back positive. Rob had a major problem — an unusual disease causing relentlessly progressive loss of brain function.

I didn't know what to say. My mind was in a daze. *This couldn't be happening — not to Rob. Surely God wouldn't let this happen to a man who had sacrificed much to study and preach His Word?* He had basically only just started his ministry — he was in the prime of life. At a time when there are so many Christian leaders who compromise the Word of God, and thus undermine its authority, my brother was totally committed to standing for its full authority. None of it seemed fair. I must admit that from an up-close human perspective, none of this seemed to make sense.

Granted, Rob sinned . . . but not horrendous kinds of sins, not the kinds of sins that we see in the lives of lawless pagans — who often live long, carefree, and healthy lives. He was a man who sought God. Not only had he trusted the Lord Jesus Christ (the Creator of the universe) for salvation, but he had also dedicated his life to preaching God's Word. Even though Rob, like everyone else, was under the condemnation of death, surely a God of love wouldn't let some terrible disease inflict a person like him? How could that be fair? Here was my brother, one of God's faithful children, afflicted with a disease most of us don't even want to think about — a disease that caused him to lose his mind and die slowly, while others lived on in health. My struggles echoed those of David, who in Psalm 73:12–14 said:

> Behold, these are the wicked; and always at
> ease, they have increased in wealth. Surely in vain
> I have kept my heart pure, and washed my hands
> in innocence; for I have been stricken all day long,
> and chastened every morning.

Fueled by frustration and feelings, these thoughts were tossed around in my mind. But as I continued to stand back and see the big picture (putting our specific situation into the broader biblical perspective), I was led to a conclusion that reflected God's perspective rather than my human one. Did Rob deserve to suffer the way he did? The answer is "yes."

When you think about it from a Christian perspective, we *all* deserve much, much more than the suffering afflicting Rob. Because of our rebellious condition, we don't even deserve to live. But God didn't annihilate us, He has allowed us to live — while at the same time giving us a taste of what life is like without God.

We sin because we want independence from God; we want to be our *own* god. That was the hook of the temptation in the Garden: *Eat of the fruit and you shall be like God.* That alone should have been a complete and immediate death sentence for Adam (or for us as we make similar choices). If God didn't show merciful restraint, rather than fully granting our desire to be free from Him, *we wouldn't even exist.* Colossians 1:16–17 says:

> For by Him all things were created, both in the heavens and on earth, visible and invisible . . . all things have been created by Him and for Him. He is before all things, *and in Him all things hold together* (emphasis added).

God has obviously withdrawn some of that sustaining power so that creation is no longer held in a perfect state but sustained in an imperfect state. Now our bodies and everything around us falls apart eventually. We are actually living in a world where we can taste what it is like to live without God —mutations, death, suffering, etc. This is a necessary consequence of rebellion against our Creator. We *do* deserve what befalls us. We *don't* deserve what God has done for us. We don't deserve even the life we do have.

Why Doesn't He Heal?

Sometimes, when I called my mother to see how Rob was doing, Mum would tell me how she'd been up all night praying that God would heal him. "I believe God can heal him," she would say. "Don't you believe that?"

Yes, I too believed God could heal Rob. God can do anything. And over the years I've known of several verifiable situations where God's supernatural healing was obvious. In his sermon, however, Rob also carefully documented a slew of healing hoaxes that have permeated Christianity and embarrassed the Church.[1] While God *can* heal, it certainly does not mean that He *will* . . . and we best not assume His intent in any situation.

As we sought balance and focus regarding this issue, Rob's own words spoke to us again through the taped sermon. As you consider what he stated, you will see his

sincere devotion to the Lord and his intense burden to
challenge people to focus on Him and Him only:

> In many churches today, the focus is on our
> ailments, on our illnesses and on our sicknesses,
> and so on. But the problem is that when that is
> the focus . . . we are focusing on ourselves rather
> than focusing on the Lord Jesus Christ and rather
> than focusing on what the Bible is actually saying
> and telling us. Now you see, I am not for a mo-
> ment suggesting that the Lord can't heal or can't
> bring miraculous things in people's lives, I am not
> suggesting that for a moment. . . . The miraculous
> sign that the Lord gives us (and the sign that we
> constantly need to be seeking and focusing on) is
> the sign where the Lord Jesus came into this world
> and gave up His life and shed His blood that you
> and I could be drawn to Christ. He rose from the
> dead. This is the greatest sign in the history of this
> world and it will be the greatest sign until the Lord
> Jesus comes again. This is the great miracle: Christ
> came into the world to give His life.

Did We Lack Faith?

Faith is an indispensable element of the Christian
life, important in all aspects of our belief and hope.
Some have wrongly assumed, however, that healing is

dependent on our level of faith; they claim that if we had enough faith, we would always be healed. But is that the case? It sure wasn't for the apostle Paul. While a man of incredible faith, he recognized the humbling gift of illness in his own life — even though he prayed in faith for its removal:

> . . . for this reason, to keep me from exalting myself, there was given to me a thorn in the flesh, a messenger of Satan to torment me. . . . Concerning this I implored the Lord three times that it might leave me (2 Corinthians 12:7–8; NAS95).

Robert addressed Paul's situation in his sermon, referring also to the suffering of Job:

> Job was afflicted, where the Lord allowed the devil to afflict Job . . . and there the Lord allowed the devil to afflict Paul . . . and whatever this thorn was, it was incredibly painful. The word "torment" comes from the word "buffeted" and it means "a fist crushing bones." It means this: Whatever Paul had, it was brutally painful. I don't know what it was, whether it was his eye, or whatever it be, it was incredibly painful. In 2 Corinthians 12:8, Paul stated, "Three times I pleaded with the Lord to take it away from me." Three times he asked the

Lord to take it away. *But it didn't happen.* It didn't go, so the question you see that I must ask, the question I have to ask the apostle Paul is, "Paul, why didn't you have enough faith? That must be the whole problem, Paul. You didn't work up enough faith. You didn't believe enough, that is your problem." So many people face exactly that sort of aspect today; so many people. By the way, I want you to notice that Paul does not bind the devil; nowhere does he rebuke, nowhere does he cast this out, nowhere!

When Robert said that "So many people face that sort of aspect today," I wonder if he had any idea that he would soon be one of those "so many people." While many people gathered around us in this time of need, some cruelly suggested that there was a lack of faith on Robert's part and our part, and that that's why Robert had not been healed.

Yet again, we see many biblical examples where faithful people were not healed. In 2 Timothy 4:20, for example, we read, "Erastus remained at Corinth, but Trophimus I left sick in Miletus." I'm sure Paul prayed for Trophimus, and no one is condemned here for a lack of faith causing this man's sickness. The same Paul through whom God at other times had miraculously healed the lame — even raised the dead — left Trophimus knowing

✝

that, under the sovereignty of God, his ministry would not in any way be thwarted. However, Paul also recognized that sickness is a "normal" part of this life.

In 2 Corinthians 1:8, Paul takes this point further as he says, "We despaired even of life." Paul knew toward the end of his life that he would probably be martyred. Certainly, God could have stopped this, and no doubt Paul prayed concerning this matter, but he also recognized that in a world where "men loved the darkness rather than the light" (John 3:19), death was also a "normal" course of events.

Please understand that this does not mean that we shouldn't seek medical help or should just "resign" ourselves to death. This is a position Rob never took. This is certainly not to say that we shouldn't pray for physical healing either (James 5 actually commands us to do so). Rob acknowledged that God can bring healing and at times does so for His purposes. However, this is certainly not the normal course of events in today's world. The "normal" course of events, as Rob has clearly stated, is this:

> People suffer all sorts of trauma in their fallen state. Even if God heals someone physically, eventually they still will have to succumb to the effects of sin and the curse on their physical body. . . . The Bible makes it clear, including through the actions of Christ himself, that local, temporary

efforts to alleviate the Curse, such as healing of sicknesses, binding up wounds, and so on, are to be encouraged.

The normal effects of the Curse will always be realized; that's what we are to expect. Sooner or later, through disease, decay, or disaster, the bodies we live in will die and perish. "For you are dust, and to dust you shall return" (Genesis 3:19).

What Then Do We Do?

It's impossible to describe all that I experienced as I continued to listen to my brother's voice through the tape player. His words were so distinct, his voice so confident, and his instruction so urgent. The irony was so amazing. Here he was, describing the reasons behind the very situation he was in, laying a foundation through Genesis to explain his condition. Then, as he moved into the application section of the sermon, it was as if he began to instruct me personally, advising me of specific ways I could respond as I navigated my way through the issues that his illness had caused us to face. Without in any way negating the fact that we pray for physical healing, Rob challenged his congregation (and us) this way:

> I suggest that when we are talking to somebody who is sick, that we need to restructure our terminology, that we might go to the person and

say, "Brother, sister, I want you to know that we love you dearly. I want you to know we can see how much you are sick, and we are really praying to the Lord for you. We are just praying for you, really praying. And we want you to know how much we want to help you, and we want to come and help you. I'd like to pray with you. We are going to bring some meals for your family. We want to help you."

Since Rob recognized that sickness is a normal part of this life (even though we can ask God for healing), he exhorted us to *encourage* the sick person, telling them that we love them and are praying for them — prayers that include asking for the strength and comfort of those being most affected. He then encouraged practical acts of service that help the suffering person and those closest to them with the burdens they face during the tribulation.

This was a good reminder for me. I had flown to Australia especially to spend time with my mother and Brenda, the boys, and the rest of the family. This time of need presented unending opportunity to encourage them and share the weight that they were all carrying. Around me, family and friends were extending helping hands in all sorts of ways to Brenda, Joshua, and Geoffrey. Each word was a clear expression of love and care;

each thoughtful act helped them with the physical demands of those days.

Sadly, many people (including many Christians) didn't know how to handle the situation. Personally, I think this was because they didn't have a full understanding (like Rob did) of the sin-cursed nature of this world, and how we should view life through God's "eyes." Without that foundation, they didn't know how to cope with a man of God like Rob being in such terrible physical condition. Robert's disease caused him to lose considerable self-awareness and depleted his ability to communicate. It took a lot of physical work to be around him . . . but for those who didn't have a biblical world view, it took a lot of mental work, too. Without a scriptural understanding of what was going on, people felt very awkward in his presence.

Without a big picture perspective, some avoided the situation altogether, while others gave in to false hopes or false fears. These were all things that didn't reflect the truth, the truth that what Robert was going through was actually "normal."

As I continued to listen to Rob's sermon tape, my mind had found closure on so many issues. Objectively, I now had specific confirmation to the answers that I had found through the big picture. Rob, too, was convinced that *sin* was the answer to the question "How do you explain death and suffering in a world where an all-powerful, loving, and just God exists." Rob's message had also addressed many other issues regarding healing and "fairness" — issues that we would continue to face in the closing weeks of his life. But the closure for me was more than just theological or philosophical; it was deeply personal. Hearing Rob's voice again, and receiving the message that God had prepared years before for him to give to me began to set my soul at peace.

God's Word had answered the deepest questions we were facing on earth. What God had created was originally very good and had become deeply corrupted and contaminated by sin. God has graciously allowed us to continue to live . . . sometimes even extending life through supernatural healing. But because of sin, we all face illness, disease, and a certain death; that's the new norm on this earth.

But what happens after that? What are we to expect as we pass from this earth into eternity? God's Word, starting in Genesis, shows us that God has a plan for us beyond the grave as well.

QUESTIONS FOR GROUP DISCUSSION:

1. What would you say are the general expectations that people have who live in your neighborhood? How do they think life should work out? Where did they get these ideas?

2. Consider a situation that you would consider very "unfair." Whose fault was it? In light of both personal sin and the general sinfulness of the fallen world, would you say the person deserved it?

3. Read 2 Corinthians 12:6–10. Why do you think Paul was not healed in this situation? What do you think he meant when he said, "When I am weak, then I am strong."

QUESTIONS FOR PERSONAL REFLECTION:

1. Anger often reveals expectations. When our expectations and desires are not fulfilled, we tend to get mad. What situations make you frustrated and angry? What does this emotion reveal about your expectations?

2. In light of the fallen world we live in and the consequences of personal sin, should you change some of the things you anticipate you will get out of life? If you did change these expectations, how might your life be different?

BIBLE VERSES FOR CONTEMPLATION AND MEMORIZATION:

Genesis 3:16–19
John 16:33

Endnote

1. For his documentation on the subject of false "faith" healers, Rob quoted extensively from the book *The Experience Trap* by Kel Willis (Burwood, N.S.W.: Christian Growth Ministries Pub., 1996).

CHΔPᛏER FIVE

Yet you do not know what your life will be like tomorrow. You are just a vapor that appears for a little while and then vanishes away... But as it is, you boast in your arrogance
(James 4:14–16).

Beyond the Grave

Sometimes facing reality can be quite discouraging. It's disillusioning when we see that life is not what we thought it would be, not what we had hoped for or expected. Inside, we all harbor an innate desire for Eden — a world of security, intimacy, and provision. . . . But such a world no longer exists. Yet within the context of the fallen world around us, we can look forward to a peace and joy that supersedes our sin-tainted circumstances.

In John 16:33, Christ himself said:

> These things I have spoken to you, that in Me you
> may have peace. In the world you have tribulation,
> but take courage; I have overcome the world.

While the original creation was perfect, it has now been corrupted by sin and reels in confusion in a vacuum of truth. Thankfully, God has not left us alone in hopelessness. Through Christ and the Cross, He has purchased and prepared a way back to life for those who are willing to receive it . . . and that's important. Actually it is *really* important, for soon enough life as we know it will end and our actions will follow us into eternity.

First the Bad News

I know things have been a little heavy up to this point, so let me give you a few uplifting excerpts from Scripture in Genesis 5:

> And Adam begat Seth . . . then he died. And
> Seth begat Enosh . . . then he died. And Enosh
> begat Kenan . . . and then died. Kenan became
> the father of Mahalelel . . . and then died.

Isn't that an uplifting passage of Scripture? If you're not picking up on this, there is a pattern here! It goes like this: *And he died . . . and he died . . . and he died.* Sure, that might not *seem* very uplifting, but in the big picture of what God has done through Christ and the Cross, it can actually be great news.

I remember a man who once took a non-Christian friend to church and pulled the pastor aside and said "Now I want you to give a positive evangelistic sermon for my friend." What did the pastor do? He preached on the genealogies in Genesis 5 — each one ending with the words ". . . and he died." This man thought, *Oh no. Oh no. . . . This is not going to reach my non-Christian friend! I wanted a passage talking about Jesus dying on the cross and so on.* But do you know what? The man's friend became a Christian because the passage kept repeating ". . . and he died . . . and he died . . . and he died." The man listened and thought, *I am going to die!* The passage challenged him so much that he made a choice to get things right with God. (You never know how the Lord's going to use various passages, do you?!)

But I want you to think about this for a moment. If you took that passage, deleted some of the names and wrote in your parents' and grandparents' names, and then wrote in *your* name on the bottom line, that would be accurate, wouldn't it! Since Adam, death has been reality for every one of our ancestors and that's the future for each one of us, isn't it? What a reminder to each one of us. Prior to the Lord's return, we will live in a world where every human *is* going to die.

That understanding gives us a different perspective as we look at things like 9/11. People told me, "Oh, I am glad I wasn't in the World Trade Center. I would have died." Well, do you know what my response was? "Don't worry, your turn will come!" I am in no way trying to take away from the horrible thing that happened that day, nor do I negate the grief countless people share over those that perished there. My point is only this: Both the Christian world view and secular-humanist world view agree that even if you were thousands of miles away from New York that day, *you will still die.*

It's important to get past the "why people die" question — and face the fact that death is a reality. While reporting on a natural disaster, I once heard a television reporter ask, "If there's a God of love, why would he let so many people and children die?" We've answered that question with a firm understanding of sin. Now we need to look past that issue to the extremely practical question that must be asked: What will happen *when* I die?

Innocence Lost

Rather than facing the reality of the grave, however, many people still get caught up in philosophical questions that keep them one step away from having to deal with their own mortality. "Why would God let so many innocent people die?" I hear this question all the time. But again, let's be honest; how many "innocent" people are there in this world? Some people might appear to be innocent compared to other people, but how many people could say they are totally innocent before God? We are descendants of Adam, born "in Adam." All have sinned and fall short of the glory of God (Romans 3:23). Nothing good dwells in our flesh (Romans 7:18). We are all dead in trespasses and sin (Romans 7:24). Without Christ, our heart is deceitful above all things and desperately wicked; there's none righteous, no not one (Jeremiah 17:9).

Honestly, there are no innocent people anywhere in the world. That's why all people will die. That's why we need to think beyond the grave. When it comes to death, it's not really a matter of "why," and it's certainly not a matter of "if." What matters is that death is imminent . . . and left to ourselves, we stand condemned before a holy God.

Looking Toward Forever

Our sin has placed us on a course away from God; if we continue in that direction on earth, we will continue in that direction after death — existing in eternal separation from God in hell, where punishment and isolation will forever be the norm. There are plenty of people who reject that biblical fact. They often ask questions such as "Why would a loving God sentence people to a horrible place like hell?" The question implies that it's God's fault. But it's not. When we correctly understand who we are as descendents of Adam, and contemplate the implications

✞

of the Fall, then we should understand that it's not God's fault at all. It's ours.

C.S. Lewis wrote that those who are in hell *will* to be there, and would be worse off in God's holy presence as unrepentants.[1] We, in Adam, separated ourselves from God through our sin, effectively saying we didn't want Him. Remember, the temptation was that we would be like Him, that we would be our own god, choosing our own right from wrong according to what seems good to us. Sin is far more than just actions; it's an act of high treason against the Creator and Sustainer of all life. God is a righteous God, and thus had to judge sin — but in reality we have sentenced ourselves to hell (eternal separation from God) by our actions to be independent of Him.

You can see the impasse this has caused: As the God of love, our Lord desires for us to be united with Him forever . . . but as the God of justice, he must punish sin and rebellion. Romans 6:23 says "the wages of sin is death," and Hebrews 9:22 says that "without shedding of blood there is no forgiveness." Yes, it is our fault that we are destined for hell and can do nothing to save ourselves, but is it possible that God, in His merciful and timeless wisdom, created a way out for us?

The First Sacrifice

The LORD God made garments of skin for Adam and his wife, and clothed them. Then the

Lord God said, "Behold, the man has become like one of Us, knowing good and evil; and now, lest he stretch out his hand, and take also from the tree of life, and eat, and live forever" — therefore the Lord God sent him out from the garden of Eden, to cultivate the ground from which he was taken (Genesis 3:21–23).

God is a righteous God. All His ways are perfect, so He had to judge sin with death. Banished from Eden where the tree of life grew, the descendents of Adam and Eve would forever know illness, suffering, and death. Prior to driving them from the Garden, however, God clothed them with garments of skin. (That's the origin of clothing by the way; the first covering of our guilt.) But I would like to suggest to you that it's even more than that. Adam and Eve's sons, Cain and Abel, knew they had to bring a sacrifice to God . . . so we know that *someone* had shown them that there needed to be a sacrifice because of sin. I believe that the very first sacrifice — the first blood sacrifice as a covering for sin — takes place right there in Genesis 3:21, where God killed an animal, and then used the skin to clothe Adam and Eve. It is the first recorded incident of *nephesh* death, the first killing of something with flesh and blood. God is the one that provided the animal; He is the one that performed the sacrifice . . . and He did it for the sinners He loved.

This first sacrifice was a picture of what was to come in Jesus Christ — a looking forward to the redemption that could be ours in Christ. It's what we would call a "proto-gospel" — a preview of Christ and what He was to do on the Cross when God himself provided the perfect sacrifice for the sins of all.

We see in this first sacrifice a picture of God's covering for the sin of Adam and Eve and a prophetic image of what is to come. . . . It's right there in Genesis 3:15 where God chastises the serpent (the devil) and tells him, "I will put enmity between you and the woman, and between your seed and her seed; He shall bruise you on the head, and you shall bruise him on the heel."

This proto-gospel and these prophecies were realized when God himself stepped into human history to become a man so He could pay the price for our sins, which was death. Through His resurrection, He proved He had victory over death, and now offers us the free gift of salvation.

> For while we were still helpless, at the right time Christ died for the ungodly. . . . But God demonstrates His own love toward us, in that while we were yet sinners, Christ died for us. Much more then, having now been justified by His blood, we shall be saved from the wrath of God through Him (Romans 5:6–9).

Therefore, just as through one man sin entered into the world, and death through sin, and so death spread to all men, because all sinned. . . . But the free gift is not like the transgression. For if by the transgression of the one the many died, much more did the grace of God and the gift by the grace of the one Man, Jesus Christ, abound to the many (Romans 5:12–15).

The whole of Romans 5 draws a vivid contrast between Adam and Christ . . . a powerful comparison between the one whose sin initiated death and the One whose death can bring us life.

This book has sought, like all publications associated with *Answers in Genesis,* to give glory and honor to God as Creator. We are convinced of the truth of the biblical record of the real origin and history of the world and mankind. Part of this real history is the bad news that the rebellion of the first man, Adam, against God's command brought death, suffering, and separation from God into this world. We see the results all around us. All of Adam's descendants are sinful from conception (Psalm 51:5) and have entered into this rebellion of sin. We therefore cannot live with a Holy God, but are condemned to separation from God. The Bible says that all are therefore subject to "eternal destruction, away from the presence of the Lord and from the glory of His power" (2 Thessalonians 1:9).

But the good news is that God has done something about it. "For God so loved the world, that He gave his only begotten Son, that whoever believes in Him should not perish, but have everlasting life" (John 3:16). Jesus Christ — though totally sinless — suffered on behalf of mankind, paying the penalty of mankind's sin — the penalty of death and separation from God.

Leviticus 17 tells us that the life of a creature is in its blood; so blood represents life and there has to be a shedding of life to pay the penalty of death. Hebrews 9:22 says, "Without shedding of blood there is no forgiveness." Indeed, sacrifices have been made since the first one in the Garden, but the blood of bulls and goats can't wash away human sin (Hebrews 10:4). Because we are not connected to the animal kingdom, human blood had to be shed . . . and it had to be perfectly sinless blood in order to sufficiently pay the price of all sin.

That's why God did the unthinkable: The Creator himself stepped into history to be one of us, to be our substitute on the Cross. We rebelled against our Holy God; we don't even deserve to exist. But God not only allows us to exist, but He also provided a way for us to come back to be with Him. Through Christ's death on the Cross, He satisfied the righteous demands of the holiness and justice of God His Father. Jesus was the perfect sacrifice; but on the third day He rose again, conquering death. All who truly believe in Him, repent of their sin, and trust in Him (rather than their own efforts), are able to come back to God and live now and for eternity with their Creator.

> He who believes in Him is not condemned, but he who does not believe is condemned already, because he has not believed in the name of the only begotten Son of God (John 3:18; NKJV).

> There is therefore now no condemnation for those who are in Christ Jesus. For the law of the Spirit of life in Christ Jesus has set you free from the law of sin and of death (Romans 8:1–2).

> Therefore, having been justified by faith, we have peace with God through our Lord Jesus Christ (Romans 5:1).

Those who accept this incredible gift of forgiveness and new life undergo a radical spiritual transformation . . . one in which they are "born again" (John 3:3). While all people are descendents of Adam and were born "in Adam," those who give their lives to God and receive His payment and forgiveness for their sins are spiritually re-born "in Christ."

> Therefore, if anyone is in Christ, he is a new creature; old things have passed away; behold, all

things have become new. Now all things are of God, who has reconciled us to Himself through Jesus Christ (2 Corinthians 5:17–18;l NKJV).

I have been crucified with Christ; and it is no longer I who live, but Christ lives in me; and the life which I now live in the flesh I live by faith in the Son of God, who loved me, and delivered Himself up for me (Galatians 2:20).

What a wonderful Savior — and what a wonderful salvation in Christ our Creator! By receiving His free gift of new life you can begin the great adventure of renewing and reclaiming His original intent for humanity, one in which you walk with Him and talk with Him as His child. His inerrant Word lays the foundation of truth upon which this new life is constructed; its timeless principles and insights are "living and active" (Hebrews 12:14). Struggles with the fallen world and sinful flesh will continue while on this earth, but beyond the grave, rather than eternal separation from Him forever, you will leave this world and your sinful body behind and enter into a perfect and pure relationship with Him in heaven.

Dear reader, if you have yet to come to Christ for forgiveness of sin and to have the assurance of eternal life, do it now before it is too late. Nothing else offers any hope, and nothing else makes sense of all of reality. This is where the "big picture" must become *your* picture. You must choose to receive His free gift of salvation. If you are having difficulty reconciling Bible/science issues, write to the nearest *Answers in Genesis* office, or check our website, www.AnswersInGenesis.org, where you'll find a wealth of information, resources, and encouragement. If you have become a Christian from reading this book, we would love for you to write and tell us; and of course, we would encourage you to commit to a strong Bible-believing church.

Let me be very straightforward with you right now. If you are rejecting God and Christ because of questions you have regarding suffering and death, it's time to get past that. As I've shown you, there are sound and reasonable answers from Scripture regarding these questions, but if you choose to dwell on these issues, basing your objections on what *you* think is right and wrong, you're going to miss the point. The point right now isn't *why* death and suffering exist, or *why* some seem to suffer more or die sooner than others . . . the point is that you *will* die, and you need to be prepared for that reality.

Christ faced these same objections in Luke 13. Someone brought up an "unjust" situation where Pilate had killed Galilean citizens and mixed their blood with his sacrifices (a hideous atrocity for sure). Jesus cut to the real issue, however, with this response:

Do you suppose that these Galileans were greater sinners than all other Galileans because they suffered this fate? I tell you, no, but unless you repent, you will all likewise perish. Or do you suppose that those eighteen on whom the tower in Siloam fell and killed them, were worse culprits than all the men who live in Jerusalem? I tell you, no, but unless you repent, you will all likewise perish (Luke 13:2–5).

Issues of "fairness" and supposed "injustice" may pester us for the rest of our lives, but the core issue that Jesus focuses on is the one we have already stated: They died. It was their time. You are going to die. Now is your time to repent and turn to the Lord. Make sure you have committed your life to Christ, for death is a reality, and what happens beyond the grave depends on your decisions in life.

QUESTIONS FOR GROUP DISCUSSION:

1. Many people have a clear understanding of the gospel, and yet do not repent and receive God's gift of salvation. What are some of the reasons this might be?

2. Do you think that concerns about the origin of suffering and death are legitimate reasons to reject the gospel? Why or why not?

3. C.S. Lewis wrote that those who are in hell *will* to be there, and would be worse off in God's holy presence as unrepentants. What do you think of that statement?

QUESTIONS FOR PERSONAL REFLECTION:

1. Contemplate James 4:13–17. Do you *really* believe this passage, or is death just a hypothetical? How would your life be different if you truly realized that the end of your life could come at any moment?

2. If you had to explain God's motives for coming to earth and dying on the cross *for you*, what would you say?

3. Can you pinpoint a time or season when you committed your life to Christ and accepted His offer of forgiveness and renewed life? If not, why not talk to God about it right now. Thank Him for dying in your place for your sins. Invite Him to come into your spirit, and commit your life to Him and His purposes.

BIBLE VERSES FOR CONTEMPLATION AND MEMORIZATION:

Understanding who you now are "in Christ" is a vital aspect of a godly life. Spend some time considering

117

each of these truths presented in God's Word. How could these truths from the Bible change your life?

1 John 1:9

Galatians 4:4-7

Ephesians 4:22-24

Ephesians 2:10

Endnotes

1. C.S. Lewis, *The Great Divorce* (New York: Simon & Schuster, 1996).

CHΔP✝ER ꙅIX

*The Spirit of the Sovereign LORD is upon me . . .
to preach good news to the poor. He has sent me to
bind up the brokenhearted, to proclaim freedom
for the captives and release from darkness for the
prisoners . . . to comfort all who mourn... to
bestow on them a crown of beauty instead of ashes*
(Isaiah 61:1–3; NIV).

Beauty from Ashes

In his book *Holy Sweat,*[1] Tim Hansel coined the phrase "turn your theology into your biography." That's an interesting concept, and by stating it, Hansel implies that our theology (what we believe about God) doesn't normally match up with our biography (the actual course of our life). This mismatch can create a great gap between our *expectations* about what we think life should be like and our *experiences* in reality. In this gap can grow the roots of great disappointment — roots that grow into the question *How do you explain death and suffering in a world where an all-powerful, loving, and just God exists?*

As we've stated earlier, the question is not just a smokescreen that unbelievers put up to avoid facing the gospel (though many do so quite frequently), it's a question believers wrestle with to a great extent as well.

For some reason, many Christians have picked up the notion that everything should begin to work out the way they want now that they have given their lives to Christ. But when reality doesn't match expectations, disappointment and disillusionment are the result.

Theologically, we know that God *is*, and we know that He is *good*. But when we look at our biography, we see a trail of pain and suffering (not exactly the way we would expect a loving Father to treat His children). So philosophically speaking, the problem of evil turns out to be a problem for the believer as well. Desperately we seek reconciliation between the pain and evil we experience and this loving God we believe in. We can now clearly see that *sin* is the root cause of suffering and death, but somehow, *this evil has to be compatible with God's goodness.*

God created everything, knows everything, is all-powerful, and exists in all places. He is also the embodiment and definer of "good." Somehow, our theology and our biography must be meshed on this point. Some people (like Turner and Darwin) change their theology in the face of difficult events. But since God is unchanging (Malachi 3:6), and the inerrant Word of God clearly tells us who He is, the only thing we can rightly change is our attitude and our perspective toward evil.

With that in mind, I'd like to turn to a well-known and well-worn passage of God's Word, Romans 8:28:

> And we know that God causes all things to work together for good to those who love God, to those who are called according to His purpose.

I bring up this portion of the Bible with some hesitancy. Too often it has been used as a superficial band-aid, slapped on gaping wounds as a quick-fix for deeply rooted pain and difficulty. These words are not some cure-all cliché to be thrown at someone who is hurting. This is the Word of God . . . something to be seriously considered and applied, recognized for what it says and also for what it does *not* say.

First, it's important to notice that the verse does *not* say that all things are good. Paul is clearly acknowledging in this passage (as he does in many, many others) that bad things exist and bad things happen. The passage simply says that "all things *work together* for good." Secondly, this passage is reserved for those "who love God and are called according to His purpose." This passage does *not* apply to those who have rejected God and are continuing to live in independence from Him. An entirely different fate awaits them.

So what this passage does say is that God causes all things — *even evil events* — to occur for reasons that are morally commendable and good. Bahnsen said this:

> If the Christian *presupposes* that God is perfectly and completely good — as Scripture requires us to do — then he is committed to evaluating everything within his experience in the light of that presupposition. Accordingly, when the Christian observes evil events or the things in the world, he can, and should, retain consistency with his presupposition about God's goodness by now *inferring* that God has a *morally good reason* for the evil that exists. God certainly must be all-powerful in order to be God; He is not to be thought of as overwhelmed or stymied by evil in the universe. And God is surely good, the Christian will profess — so any evil we find must be compatible with God's goodness. This is just to say that God has planned evil events for reasons which are morally commendable and good.[2]

Theoretically that's not too difficult to understand. Practically, however, it's often very tough to accept. When we stare evil events in the face — feeling their full weight and implications — it's difficult to believe Romans 8:28. Thankfully, we don't have to rely solely on our own biography to see that this verse is true. Numerous examples from the Bible illustrate that evil events have been planned by God to work for the good.

From Bad to Good

The account of Esther is a powerful example of God's omniscient plan that causes all things to work for good. The event takes place in the days of King Ahasuerus, who reigned from India to Ethiopia. The king was searching far and wide for a new wife to be his queen, and that's when he discovered Esther.

> Now there was a Jew in Susa the capital whose name was Mordecai . . . who had been taken into exile from Jerusalem with the captives . . . whom Nebuchanezzar the king of Babylon had exiled. And he was bringing up Hadassah, that is Esther, his uncle's daughter, for she had neither father or mother. Now the young lady was beautiful of form and face, and when her father and her mother died, Mordechai took her as his own daughter (Esther 2:5–7).

The king was initially unaware that Esther was a Jewess. But after a huge selection process, he chose her as his queen. Sometime after Esther had become queen, a

✛

wicked man named Haman plotted to have all Jews killed. Because Esther had access to the king, she alone was in the position to petition the king to save the Jews. But according to the laws of the land, if Esther approached the king on this matter, she would likely be killed.

When Mordecai sent a message to Esther (urging her to petition the king) she sent him this reply:

> All the king's servants and the people of the king's provinces know that for any man or woman who comes to the king to the inner court who is not summoned, he has but one law, that he be put to death, unless the king holds out to him the golden scepter so that he may live. And I have not been summoned to come to the king for these thirty days (Esther 4:11).

You can imagine the tension as Esther struggled with what she should do. Still, Mordecai saw beyond the initial threat. He saw not only the urgency of the situation, but he also saw God's hand in placing Esther where she was . . . and he exhorted her with these words:

> Do not think that you in the king's palace can escape any more than all the Jews. For if you remain silent at this time, relief and deliverance will arise for the Jews from another place and you and your

father's house will perish. *And who knows whether you have not attained royalty for such a time as this?* (Esther 4:13–14, emphasis added).

Mordecai not only realized the powerful position Esther was in, but also challenged Esther to think in terms of God's sovereign plan for her life. *Could it be that all the circumstances of the past — circumstances that had resulted in her being queen — were planned by God just for this vital occasion?* I'm sure Esther thought about her childhood and all that had happened to her. Then she stepped out in faith to save her people.

During that time, the king also read a record of Mordecai's past actions revealing that Mordecai had saved the king from an evil conspiracy. These events became entwined in a fascinating and twisted series of circumstances that revealed the plot in which Haman had attempted to manipulate the king to eliminate the Jewish people. When the king realized the truth, Haman ended up being sentenced to death.

I've often wondered what was going through Mordecai's mind after the Jews were saved. I'm sure he pondered the past events surrounding his niece Esther — the events that so long ago had brought them together "for such a time as this." Perhaps he and Esther understood that it was the death of Esther's parents which ultimately led to the saving of an entire nation.

The details of Esther's parents have been lost from history. Were her parents killed? Did they die at an early age from some horrible disease? We do not know. Did people look at Esther and say, "Why would God allow this beautiful little young girl to lose her parents and why would that happen?" And yet, as we now stand back and see her place in the big picture, you can see the morally commendable reasons that God had. Through the tragic death of her parents, God brought Esther into the home of Mordecai in circumstances that led to the saving of an entire group of people.

In addition to that, Esther's life and actions have been recorded and made a part of the Holy Word of God for all eternity. How many millions and millions of times has the Book of Esther been read, changing hearts and lives? At the time of her parent's death, I doubt that any-one would have imagined that God would "cause" those tragic circumstances to "work together for good." From a human perspective, it would have only seemed to be grossly unfair.

A similar situation exists with my dad and the death of my grandfather. There's no doubt that my father had an unusual love for the Bible. Years after his death, I still remember when I used to walk into the house and see him sitting in his favorite chair with his reading glasses on, a pen in his hand, and his copiously marked Bible in his lap.

Dad was a teacher, and, as a public school principal, was transferred to many different towns around the State of Queensland. Dad and Mum started Sunday schools and ran Bible studies everywhere they went. They hosted missionaries and sponsored outreach programs to reach children and adults. (In fact, it was at one of these programs in Innisfail, North Queensland, that I went forward at a meeting to make a commitment to be a missionary for the Lord.

Dad hated it when the Bible was knowingly compromised and would always stand up for what he believed, regardless of the persecution he would receive. One Sunday, for example, we were in church and the pastor preached about the boy who provided the five thousand with the few loaves and fishes. The pastor said that what happened wasn't really a miracle, but that because a little boy took out his loaves and fishes, he set a great example for the others to follow, and they then took out their own food and shared it with each other. My father was furious! At the end of the service, he led the whole family up to the pastor and began rebuking him from the Bible, proving conclusively that this was, indeed, a miracle. He would preface his statements with "It is written . . ." as he expounded on the Bible's account of this event.

Many years later, as Dad lay dying in a hospital, Robert asked him, "Dad, why did you have such a love for the Word of God? What was it that caused you to stand so strongly on Scripture?" I had never asked Dad about this, and my heart raced — I couldn't wait to hear the answer.

Dad told Rob that when he was only 16 years old, his father died. It was a great personal loss to a young lad. But because he no longer had an earthly father to turn to, he turned to his Heavenly Father, reading His Word over and over again, becoming more and more committed to its message and more and more convinced of its authority. As I listened to Rob, I became rather choked up. Yes, it made sense. Dad seemed to be always reading the Bible — he really loved God's Word, and that love emerged out of tragic circumstances.

This love overflowed into our family, influencing our entire upbringing. My dad's passion for the Bible is one of the major reasons Rob had such a love for the Word of God and worked so hard to tell others about the gospel. (Rob was also a "chip off the old block," as people say.) He was like Dad in so many ways, never compromising the Scriptures, always standing up for what he believed was right, regardless of the consequences. And there's no doubt in my mind that I would not have started *Answers in Genesis* (a ministry that now reaches multi-thousands of people on a daily basis) if it weren't for my father and mother's stand on the Word of God. Who would have thought that a young teenager's father's death would be used by God to cause millions of people to hear about God's infallible, authoritative Word and the gospel?

I've recalled these events in my mind many times over the past years, particularly as I've thought about what happened to Rob. As I pondered these things in my heart, something became very clear to me — something that has been of great comfort in the midst of terrible sorrow: God *does* cause all things to work together for good.

The death of Esther's parents and the death of my grandfather are only two examples of God using suffering, division, and death to work for a greater good. In Acts 15:39–41, we see how God used a bitter disagreement between Paul and Barnabas to cause a split in their ministries — a division which resulted in both Cyprus and Syria being reached with the gospel. Similarly, persecution faced by the Antioch church was used to disperse them throughout the surrounding region, preaching about Christ as they went (Acts 14:5–7). The story of Joseph, of course, is a classic example of God using the sinful intent of his brothers for great good. Read this amazing story for yourself in Genesis 39–50. You'll see the unmistakable hand of God leading Joseph into great injustices in order to bring him to a position where he saved countless lives from starvation. When he faced the brothers who had caused him such strife, Joseph actually comforted them with these words:

> Do not be afraid, for am I in God's place?
> And as for you, you meant evil against me, but

God meant it for good in order to bring about this present result, to preserve many people alive (Genesis 50:19–20).

By anyone's standards, Joseph endured great hardship and betrayal (in spite of the fact that he continually chose to live uprightly in all situations). Looking back it's clear to see that God had planned the evil against him for morally commendable and good reasons.

Sometimes the good that comes out of suffering is quite incidental to the circumstances, proving that God shows infinite creativity in causing all things to work for good. Think about the suffering of Job. While Job was dealing with the onslaught of suffering and loss in his life, I'm sure that the last thing he was thinking about was the possibility that a book would one day be written outlining all the details of what happened to him . . . a book that was to be incorporated into the holy written Word of God, used to teach generation after generation necessary truths that God wanted us to understand.

I often quote the Book of Job in my talks on Genesis. In Job 40:15, while using creation as proof of His power and control, God describes an animal that could very well have been a dinosaur. It's circumstantial evidence that man and dinosaurs co-existed, and thousands of children and adults have benefited from this teaching as an important piece in the big picture of history.

One of my favorite verses of the Bible is also found in Job 38:4, "Where were you when I laid the foundation of the earth? Tell me, if you have understanding." God rebuked Job with this question when he questioned God's role in the ill that had befallen him. I teach children and adults all over the world to ask the same question to secularists who claim that life has evolved over millions of years: *"Were you there?"* I have heard so many testimonies from parents who say this has helped their children combat the false teaching regarding origins and the age of the earth. As a result of Job, many children have asked evolutionary scientists, "Were you there?" — and then they watch them fumble for a response!

From the Vantage Point of Time

We are not told of the events surrounding the death of Esther's parents. Perhaps they died of some horrible disease or were tragically killed by the invading army that forced the Israelites into exile. At the time of their death, some Jews might have questioned why God would allow a young girl to lose both her parents. Maybe even Mordecai questioned in his heart why God would allow such a seemingly terrible situation to befall such a lovely young girl as Esther.

At the time of the tragedy, no human being could foresee the future; yet God was working out a plan beyond what anyone could have imagined. Esther was being placed in circumstances such that she would be used

✝

by God to save the Jewish people . . . but no one could see it at the time.

When my father's father died, those close to the situation grieved greatly. Some may have even commented that it didn't seem fair that a young lad like my dad would be left on this earth without his father. Some might even have been angry at God, or perhaps some might have mocked Christians who believed in a holy, loving, and just God in the midst of such a situation.

However, many years later, we can look back and see the good that God worked — good that no one would have even come close to guessing at the time. The situation that caused my father to turn to his Heavenly Father (and ultimately igniting his passion for the Bible) resulted in a godly family who stood on the authority of the Word of God. Rob became a preacher of the Word. I was instrumental in founding a ministry that has grown around the world. Others in the family have been involved in various Christian ministries. All of this put new meaning into the verse of Scripture many often quote when tragedy strikes, "For My thoughts are not your thoughts, neither are your ways My ways, declares the LORD" (Isaiah 55:8).

The contemporary worship song *In His Time* puts these truths to music with these words:

> In His time; in His time
> He makes all things beautiful in His time.

Lord, please show me every day
As You're teaching me Your way
That You do just what You say
In Your time.

Nowhere is this timing more evident than in the events surrounding the death and resurrection of Jesus Christ. Without question, his brutal death on the Cross was the most unjust event in the history of all humanity . . . an absolutely sinless and perfect man beaten to a pulp, hung with spikes through His own flesh, left gasping in the hot sun while the jeers of the mocking crowd filled the air. . . .

Those closest to Him hid in fear and disillusionment. The hopes of the masses (who thought Him to be the chosen Savior) were buried with His broken and bloody body, sealed in despair as the rock was rolled across the opening of the tomb. From anyone's perspective it was a horrible, devastating event — but time would prove differently.

Just three days later the *unthinkable* — the *unimaginable* — had happened. The tomb was empty and rumors circulated of the impossible: *He was alive!* The sunrise that Sunday morning revealed that the Son had risen. As the reality of the news was confirmed by His appearances, the whole of human history was altered forever.

Still in shock over their loss, the followers of Christ realized that the most evil of deaths had resulted in the greatest victory conceivable: The perfect sacrifice had been given for sin. Victory over the grave was now a possibility. A new covenant of grace and freedom replaced the bondage of legalism and slavery to religion. The price of redemption had been paid, sealing the promise of forgiveness and opening the door to an intimate relationship with the Creator once again. God had caused horrible circumstances to work together for good, and as a result the most evil of events was transformed into the most glorious of realities.

From the perspective of time and the Resurrection, we can even see *death* itself as a moral good. Death is properly called the "last enemy" (1 Corinthians 15:26). But in a strange and obvious way, it is also a blessing for mankind. Ultimately, without death, humanity would have no way of experiencing complete reconciliation with God. Confined in our bodies of sinful flesh, our separation from Him would be eternal, but for those who believe in Christ, death is the doorway into a glorious future.

Peace in the Midst

Yes, Romans 8:28 is far from cliché. Those who are willing to consider the deeper implications of this truth, looking to examples in the Bible for support, will find the hope and faith to carry on in the midst of suffering and death. That has certainly been the case for me . . . even with my brother Robert. The circumstance behind his illness and the loss caused by his death sent shock waves through my soul. But I believe that we will see God work this for good, both now and from the perspective of eternity.

In many ways, I can see it already. Rob's story has been read by many thousands in a previously published book called *Walking Though Shadows*. Hundreds of thousands have been touched by his example as I have spoken around the world. Many people have written to me to tell me that they have read many books on death and suffering . . . but they say that Robert's story has helped them because it is "real life" — down to earth reality — that is dealt with head-on with the Bible, starting in the Book of Genesis.

Already, I realize that my brother Robert has ministered more to people in his death than he did in his life. Lord willing, many thousands more will read this book as well, finding answers, hope, and eternal salvation. Was his death "untimely" and "terrible"? Most certainly. But the God who is in the business of taking evil and using it for good has orchestrated it for reasons that are clearly morally commendable.

Even though it doesn't stop the grief — and I must admit I still heave a sigh and shake my head in disbelief — it has been a great comfort to be reminded that God is still working through the circumstances surrounding Rob's illness and death. Maybe something even greater than Esther's situation could come out of this — who knows?

✝

God's Word is clear, and examples from the Bible and contemporary life are plentiful. With a little faith we can begin to see good in many of the circumstances we face in this fallen world . . . and that faith gives hope and perspective.

Though it is often difficult to see the good while the bad events are happening, it doesn't take too much imagination to see the *potential* for good in all that happens, particularly when we look not just at the outward circumstances, but when we focus on how God uses the outward struggles to conform us to Christ on the inside. Almost always, the good He is causing becomes more evident when we are willing to wait so we can look back from the vantage point of time passage.

In most situations, when we look at evil with the big picture in mind, God's working for good will be visible — even when we can only glimpse small slivers of His light in the midst of the darkness. But what are we to do when we can't see the good at all? In those times we must bend the knee before our sovereign God, trusting that from the perspective of eternity His goodness in the midst of the evil will be revealed.

QUESTIONS FOR GROUP DISCUSSION:

1. If, indeed, God uses the suffering and death of some individuals to bring blessings to others, do you think

He is being fair? Why or why not? Can you give examples?

2. What situations can you think of where God caused something to work for good, even though it was evil? Use both contemporary and biblical examples. Was His goodness apparent at the time of the event?

3. When people face suffering and death, how might their emotional response (depression, anger, joy, peace, etc.) reveal their level of belief in the truths of Romans 8:28?

QUESTIONS FOR PERSONAL REFLECTION:

1. Many times, the good that God is working out through difficult circumstances results in inner changes of character and faith that make us more like Christ. In what ways has the suffering and death you've experienced resulted in inner change? In most situations, do you tend to reject or embrace these changes?

2. What current situations are you facing that seem to be evil or wrong? Are you able to see God's goodness at work, or do you think it will take the perspective of time to see the result of His purpose?

3. Are you willing to accept by faith the suffering and death as something that God can (and is) working out for good? If so, spend some time praying, thanking Him for every circumstance that surrounds you.

BIBLE VERSES FOR CONTEMPLATION AND MEMORIZATION:

2 Corinthians 4:7–18

James 1:2, 12–18

Endnotes
1. Tim Hansel, *Holy Sweat* (Dallas, TX: Word Publishing, 1987).
2. G.L. Bahnsen, *Always Ready — Directions for Defending the Faith* (Nacogdoches, TX: Covenant Media Press, 2002), p. 171–172.

Bowing the Knee

I n the course of the Christian life, seasons emerge
that push the boundaries of our belief in the goodness of God, causing doubt about His willingness
and/or ability to truly "work all things for good." War,
famine, the loss of a loved one, financial concerns, divorce,
a wayward child, bankruptcy, physical disability . . . anything that threatens the things that we feel are essential to
a meaningful life expose the vulnerability of human faith.

Situations that appear to be terminal — those with no hope of healing or reconciliation — hit home the hardest. Though our lives may be filled with belief and conviction in God, in each of our hearts there comes a point where "the good" cannot be imagined; in every soul there are boundaries to faith . . . and certain circumstances can push us beyond those limits into a place where doubt and despair rule.

King David, the writer of the majority of the Psalms, was no stranger to this place. His words regularly describe hopelessness, depression, and — perhaps worst of all — the sense that God had abandoned him. Consider, for example, Psalm 44:23–24:

> Arouse Yourself, why do you sleep, O Lord? Awake, do not reject us forever. Why do you hide your face and forget our affliction and our oppression? For our soul has sunk down into the dust; our body cleaves to the earth (NAS95).

The situations that strike at our souls the most powerfully are usually the ones that are closest to our hearts: the issues of "life" that challenge our core beliefs about what is "right," the dreams that we don't even know we have, the expectations that lie central to our hopes, the tragedies that reveal our true beliefs about what should be. When circumstances press against these issues, our faith (as tattered as it may be at the moment) becomes vital for spiritual survival.

During the last days that I had with my brother, I held his hand tightly, but my faith clung desperately to God. "Lord," I said quietly, "I don't understand. He wants to tell them about You — why can't he do that? Why have You let this happen to him? It just doesn't make sense to me." As I despairingly looked at Rob, my mind traced the circumstances that had brought him to this place. It seemed like such an inappropriate end, so contrary to where we thought life would take him. It all appeared to be a total loss compared to how we thought God would use him.

As I sat at his side, my mind flashed back to the days when Robert was a successful bank manager. Through his upright character and dedicated work, he was "climbing the ladder of success" rather quickly. He had a great future in this financial institution, already enjoying a secure job with an excellent salary and many other benefits. But deep inside, Rob was wrestling with his real passion . . . a passion to preach. Just like our father, he loved the Word of God. It greatly distressed him to see preachers who did not believe the Bible regularly compromising its content and authority. Rob was deeply involved in his local church and he began lay preaching. In preparation, he read and reread sermons by some of the greats like Martyn Lloyd-Jones and Charles Haddon

Spurgeon . . . and all the while his desire to be in full-time ministry grew.

During that time, my wife and I went full-time into the creation ministry now known as *Answers in Genesis*. Rob and his wife, Brenda, often gave us much-needed financial support. In those days the ministry was very small and finances were rather scarce. Rob and Brenda's financial support helped us more than they realized, providing for our most basic needs through those financially trying years.

As the burden on Rob to preach increased, he believed God had definitely called him to leave the bank and go to a theological college so he could study God's Word and become a teacher of the Bible. He and his family sacrificed much so he could earn this theological degree. They moved to Sydney, a very expensive place to live in Australia. To keep expenses down, they rented a house that was part of a chicken farm on the outskirts of this great city. The first time I visited them I was somewhat shocked at the horrible smell from thousands and thousands of chickens. I'm not sure I could have put up with it.

Rob spent many hours a day commuting by train, bus, or car. Every possible moment during the commute was spent studying and preparing sermons. Soon, the money Rob and Brenda had saved from his years at the bank was gone, but my wife and I were now in a position to support Rob and his family financially, just as they had done for us.

. Rob studied hard . . . a seemingly unending string of long days and short nights. But he was a good student and his reputation was growing as an effective communicator of the Word of God. When his formal education was finally complete, we gave Rob a complete set of Spurgeon's works as a graduation present.

Our regular phone conversations now focused on what his next step should be. He wanted to find a church where he could reach out to the community. He also had a burden to reach Muslims and students for Christ. Underneath it all was his intense burden to preach the gospel of Christ. The bottom line was that he just wanted to reach everyone he could with the message of salvation.

After considering a number of offers, he was led to take up a position as pastor in a church on Australia's Gold Coast, one of the most pagan areas of Australia. I still remember the day he invited me along as he visited with the head deacon of this church. Rob was excited, *really* excited. His passion was developing into a specific vision for his ministry. Not far from the church was a major university and he saw great potential for reaching the students there. The church was in a very needy community, desperately in need of the gospel. As his vision clarified, he saw how this small church in the middle of it all could be used by God to make a difference.

✝

Once he was at the church, Rob threw his heart and soul into his ministry. He continued to study hard. He taught the Word of God verse-by-verse and applied it practically in today's world. Rob also had a special gift for playing the piano. After playing for the hymns and choruses, he would then get up and teach the Word of God. Brenda was deeply involved in the Sunday school and other outreaches, and the church began to grow. Some people who visited the Gold Coast for holidays heard that they could hear the Word of God taught uncompromisingly at Rob's church, so they would come and bring others. Rob's church also hosted the American tourists that my wife and I brought over each year for a special tour of Australia. Rob would have me preach, and the church would provide lunch for the tourists. What great memories.

But it all began to fall apart just when Rob's ministry was having great effect . . . after all the sacrifice and "blood, sweat, and tears," when he was beginning to fulfill the vision and burden he had for years . . . and just as things seemed to be blessed and moving ahead.

It was hard on all of us, but it was particularly hard on my mother. The terminal diagnosis, watching his mind and body decay before her eyes, preparing for the funeral . . . I think what she went through can only be understood by others who have had to bury a child, and the situation stretched her faith beyond the point where she could even begin to imagine any good that might come out of this.

"I know God is in control. I know this is a sin-cursed world. I understand all that. But I still don't understand why this would happen to him," she would cry out. "It doesn't seem to make sense! He worked so hard and preached so well. Why?" During one of my many phone calls with Mum, she said in her grief, "It doesn't seem fair. He was such a man of God who loved and preached God's Word. There are all these people who compromise the Bible, and atheists who attack it. Why did this happen to such a person as Robert?"

We were all in the here-and-now, grieving over a situation that was hard to explain in the context of a loving God as described in the Bible. If Rob had been killed in a traffic accident or contracted some deadly disease like cancer, it would have been a terrible shock, and many would have grieved greatly (and we all would have probably asked many of the same questions), but somehow, this disease seemed particularly cruel. The very gift of communication the Lord had given to him was taken away, and it was as if he was then put on the rack to be slowly tortured to death while family and friends were (if possible) tortured even more. All we could do was watch as helpless spectators, groping for answers.

As family and friends, we wrestled hard with the questions. Why would God allow this? Why did He

✝

cause it? It just didn't seem right from our perspective. There are some people that will try to put you on a guilt trip if you ask those kinds of questions, insinuating that you don't have faith in God. We had faith, for certain, but it was being seriously tested. We're humans, and I believe we can ask those questions. We did as a family, and I did as a brother — I admit it. In the hardest moments of those dark days we all had to learn to stand back and say, "God is God," and then stand aside and let Him be God.

But for Mum it seemed much worse than that; this was her son. In the regular order of things, it should have been him comforting her as she lay on the threshold of death, not the other way around. Added to this was the fact that he was leaving behind a wife and two boys in those teenage formative years — years in which the father plays such an important role in guiding their children to adulthood. So not only did Mum struggle as a mother, but she struggled as a grandmother as well.

One time her frustration overflowed and she said, "I don't understand it. The liberal pastor down the street who teaches against the Bible as the inerrant Word of God is as healthy as an ox. And look at my son who stood on the authority of the Word of God and he is suffering a horrible brain disease!"

I said, "But Mum, you have got to remember something: What's happened to Robert is going to happen to the liberal pastor. He is going to die." I even shared with her what I was learning from the tape of Robert's sermon. I said "Mum, Robert himself said that death and suffering and disease are normal in an abnormal world and we live in an abnormal world because of sin."

I went over all the Bible verses with Mum about the sovereignty of God and about the Jesus of the Bible being in control. We looked at Romans 8:28 and how all things work together for good and that God's ways are higher than ours, and so on. . . . But she knew all that. It wasn't that her *mind* didn't understand, it just seemed that her *heart* could not withstand it. Yes, it was difficult for those of us who called him brother, husband, and father; but our circumstances were even more ominous for the one who called him son. Her own body had harbored Robert's tiny growing form. She was the one who held him to her breast as he took his first breaths . . . now she was holding him again in her arms as he breathed his last.

What is one to do in such times when faith is stretched thin and circumstances bear down hard? In such times there is no other choice but to bow the knee before God and place the remaining trust that He gives back at His feet.

During the toughest of times, we must fall back on a simple and powerful truth: God is God; we are not. God is the One (the only One) who determines what is right and what will be or not be. Our place is one

✝

of submission and obedience — regardless of the pain, regardless of the confusion.

The Book of Isaiah deals with these issues extensively in Isaiah 45:6–7, 9–10:

> I am the LORD, and there is no other, the One forming light and creating darkness, causing well being and creating calamity; I am the LORD who does all these. . . . Woe to the one who quarrels with his Maker — an earthenware vessel among the vessels of earth! Will the clay say to the potter, "What are you doing?" Or the thing you are making say, "He has no hands?" Woe to him who says to a father, "What are you begetting?" Or to a woman, "To what are you giving birth?"

When the dark times come, God offers no apologies and gives few explanations — and He takes responsibility for all that is taking place. *I the Lord do all these things. Pour out your heart, if you wish, but don't argue. I'm God, you are not. Period. You have no clue about what I am doing and what will come of it.*

Yes, God is the one who raises up kingdoms and destroys them. He's in charge of those sorts of things. He is a sovereign God and so nothing happens that He doesn't know about. As one of my friends said, "God has yet to make His first mistake, because God is in total control."

That's not a cop-out; that's simply allowing God to be God. Make no mistake on this point. God is very firm. He is who He is, and He has absolutely no obligation to us to change anything according to our desires, nor should He be compelled to alter His plans to pander to our feelings.

God is God; we are not. Because of that, we have little choice but to pour out our hearts to Him in full honesty and then make a definitive decision to recognize God for who He is. Then we must humbly bow before Him and His purposes in faith. Evanell Janousek wrote this poem in 1970, reflecting both her feelings and her decision to submit:

> "Why?"
> A question I ask when I don't understand
> A problem unsolved.
> With outstretched hands I plead for relief
> From suffering and strife,
> Calling to Him who has given me life,
> Knowing he will listen
> To my troubled plea.
> "Not my will, but Thine. My trust is in thee."

David repeats this same pattern many times in the Psalms: an honest outpouring of his heart . . . followed by recognition of God's character . . . followed by a decision to submit and worship in the midst of suffering, danger, and death. This is the pattern we see in the Book of Job as well. Everything that Job cares about is taken from him — everything. In its place he is stricken with suffering and physical agony. His friends gather round to figure out his problem (None of them got it right, by the way. They never did find out what was happening behind the scenes . . . and they would have been of much more help had they kept their mouths shut and tried to serve Job in some tangible way.)

The conversation between Job and his friends is punctuated with sporadic outbursts by Job regarding his condition, as He questions God's motives and actions. He was ready to demand of God an explanation: *Why this? Why that? Why did you let this happen to me? You know I demand to speak to you!*

In chapter 38, God breaks His silence with words that are as piercing as they are true:

> Then the LORD answered Job out of the whirlwind and said, "Who is this that darkens counsel by words without knowledge? Now gird up your loins like a man. . . . Where were you when I laid the foundation of the earth? Tell Me, if you have understanding, who set its measurements, since you know? Or who stretched the line on it? On what

were its bases sunk? Or who laid its cornerstone"
(Job 38:1–6).

You can feel the sting of the rebuke. But even to a
man grieving from the loss of all of his children and suffering from open sores, God softens none of the truth
with sympathy or explanation. As we read chapters 38
through 41, God continues to grill Job with a series of
questions. They are questions with obvious answers and
God uses them to put Job sternly back into his place
in the divine order. *Do you know this, Job? What about
this. . . ?* God uses example after example to finally bring
Job to the point in Job 42 where we read:

> Then Job replied to the LORD: "I know that you
> can do all things; no plan of yours can be thwarted.
> You asked, 'Who is this that obscures my counsel
> without knowledge?' Surely I spoke of things I did
> not understand, things too wonderful for me to
> know. You said, 'Listen now, and I will speak; I
> will question you, and you shall answer me.' My
> ears had heard of you but now my eyes have seen
> you. Therefore I despise myself and repent in dust
> and ashes" (Job 42:1–6; NIV).

These are the words of a son who finally recognized
his place before his Father, and bowed the knee to His

complete and sovereign authority over all things. God is God; Job is not. Job acknowledged (as we must) that compared to what God knows, he knew nothing . . . and he repented of his human arrogance, totally submitting his life to the all-knowing, all-powerful God of the universe. Job learned the lesson the hard way, but he learned it nonetheless. Finally, he recognized the truth of Isaiah 55:8–9:

> "My thoughts are not your thoughts, neither are your ways My ways," declares the LORD. "For as the heavens are higher than the earth, so are My ways higher than your ways, and My thoughts than your thoughts."

What did Job recognize? Job recognized that he was just dust. Compared to God, he was nothing but a finite and foolish human being. He recognized that God is God, and that He knew what He was doing — even when Job was entirely incapable of understanding. And that's really the answer at the end of the Book of Job. *Don't ask why. Let God be God.* God never did reveal what was behind Job's suffering and loss. As far as we know, God offered no apology and no explanation. Only when he stepped into eternity would Job finally learn *why* God had ordained such a hideous season of suffering and death.

✝

Don't ask why. Let God be God. Bend your knee in submission, obedience, and worship. This is the answer to the issue of death and suffering during the seasons when our faith is stretched to its limit and then pushed beyond.

I praise the Lord for the faith my mother showed during her season of darkness and doubt. She pleaded and pleaded in tears with the Lord to intervene for Rob. I praise the Lord even more that, even though Rob's condition continued to worsen, my mother's faith and trust in God did not wane, but actually grew. In spite of what she could see, in spite of the pain and agony that tore at her heart, she recognized that God was God and she was not. He was good, and was in total control of the situation. And though He chose, according to His eternal purposes, not to intervene and heal, Mum knew that He cared, that He was there, and that He heard the prayers of a grieving mother.

In his taped sermon, Rob preached about Job, but he could just as well have been preaching about himself:

> You know that we must realize that Job's suffering was part of God's plan. That's what it was. It must also be true for many people today who suffer so badly, and through it all, you see Job learned the necessity of submitting to the Lord's sovereign purpose, no matter what the cost might be.

Sometimes God has asked people to sacrifice greatly so that His sovereign purposes of redemption and necessary judgment could be carried out. We've already looked at how God orchestrated the death of Esther's parents in order to save the Jewish nation. We saw how the unjust treatment of Joseph was used by God to divert a famine. Ezekiel was told that for God's purposes in dealing with the Jews, his wife — whom he loved so much — was going to be taken away from him:

> Son of man, with one blow I am about to take away from you the delight of your eyes. Yet do not lament or weep or shed any tears (Ezekiel 24:16; NIV).

During trials like that, the good promised in Romans 8:28 may seem distant and far-fetched. In those moments we have two options: 1) either we walk away and deny Him, or 2) we humbly bend the knee, trusting that He will provide the faith we need to make it through. This increased faith brings us into greater intimacy and dependence on God, and this increased level of trust is one of the common purposes in the trials He places in our paths. As Rob said in his sermon, quoting J.I. Packer:

> "The ultimate reason from our standpoint why God fills our lives with troubles and perplexities

of one sort and another, is to ensure that we shall learn to hold Him fast." The reason why the Bible spends so much of its time reiterating that God is a strong rock, a firm defense, a sure refuge, and a help for the weak, is because God is bringing home to us that we are weak, both mentally and morally. We dare not trust ourselves to find or to follow the right road. God wants us to feel that our way through life is rough and perplexing so that we may learn to lean on Him. Therefore, He takes steps to drive us out of self-confidence, to trust in himself.

Here, then, we begin to see one of God's great and eternal purposes for our ongoing suffering: *Pain and death cause us to look to God in dependence — a merciful response to the independence we seek through sin.* This is, indeed, a central theme of the Word of God. As Rob taught along these lines, he would often quote passages such as 2 Corinthians 1:3–11:

> Praise be to the God and Father of our Lord Jesus Christ, the Father of compassion and the God of all comfort, who comforts us in all our troubles, so that we can comfort those in any trouble with the comfort we ourselves have received from God. For just as the sufferings of

Christ flow over into our lives, so also through Christ our comfort overflows. If we are distressed, it is for your comfort and salvation; if we are comforted, it is for your comfort, which produces in you patient endurance of the same sufferings we suffer. And our hope for you is firm, because we know that just as you share in our sufferings, so also you share in our comfort.

We do not want you to be uninformed, brothers, about the hardships we suffered in the province of Asia. We were under great pressure, far beyond our ability to endure, so that we despaired even of life. Indeed, in our hearts we felt the sentence of death. But this happened that we might not rely on ourselves but on God, who raises the dead. He has delivered us from such a deadly peril, and he will deliver us. On him we have set our hope that he will continue to deliver us, as you help us by your prayers. Then many will give thanks on our behalf for the gracious favor granted us in answer to the prayers of many (NIV).

Rob wanted people to understand that even though we have to live with the consequences of sin in this physical universe, God loves us so much that He will provide the comfort necessary for us to cope with the various situations in which we find ourselves.

Hebrews 11:1–2 says, "Faith is the assurance of things hoped for, the conviction of things not seen. For by it the men of old gained approval." Ultimately, as we read in Hebrews 11:6, "Without faith it is impossible to please God" (NIV). There will always be a faith aspect to every area of life. This is true during trials, and it is true as we study origins as well. As I lecture on the topic of creation and evolution, I explain to people that no one can scientifically *prove* creation or Noah's flood; nor can anyone *prove* evolution and millions of years, for that matter, as none of us were there to witness these events. *Both* world views require faith. However, the Bible's account of origins in Genesis does make sense of the evidence in the world around us, and observational science confirms the biblical record. For example, Genesis tells us that God created distinct kinds of animals and plants to reproduce after their own kinds. The science of genetics confirms that no new genetic information is produced from matter, and animals and plants reproduce their own kind, even though there can be great variation (even speciation) within a kind because of the variety in the genes.

This is the point: *Only the God of the Bible is omniscient, omnipotent, and omnipresent,* and the bottom line is that *we are not.* We are not going to have all the answers to everything all the time. This side of the grave, we may never know why things like Rob's sickness have happened. Only God knows. We are nothing but fallen, mortal human beings who, like Job, need to recognize that we know nothing compared to what God knows. When we can't see the good, we walk on in faith through the revealed truth of God's Word.

Submission to God is never easy, and it always goes against the nature of our sinful flesh. The challenge to repent and submit as Job did is more difficult when we feel like a victim. During difficult times, we are also likely to feel used or abandoned. In these moments of deep trial, we feel we need the comfort of God the most, yet these may be the days when we sense it the least . . . and must choose by an act of our wills to obey and submit to God's purposes. Philip Yancey comments on this type of faith:

> I hesitate to say this, because it is a hard truth and one I do not want to acknowledge, but Job stands as merely the most extreme example of what appears to be a universal law of faith. The kind of faith God values seems to develop best when everything fuzzes over, when God stays silent, when the fog rolls in.[1]

When "the fog" becomes so thick that we can't see any of the good God promises, we have no choice but to return to His written and living Word to give us the full, big picture of what is going on around us. God's Word tells us clearly where death and sickness originated. We understand we live in a fallen world. Each of us needs to recognize that we are sinful creatures living under a Curse because of sin, and that death for every human being is both inevitable and immanent. Through Christ and the Cross, every person can be spiritually healed, but total healing won't come until we leave this sin-cursed universe. Yet here and now, God has a sovereign plan far greater than we could imagine, but we may not be able to see it or understand it at all. We don't know everything — in fact, we know *nothing* compared to God.

The question, then, becomes this: Do we put our faith in the Word of an all-powerful God, who knows everything and has always been there? Or do we place our faith in the words of fallible humans who don't know everything, who haven't always been there, and whose values and subjective thinking lead only to fatalism? The answer to that question is *repentance* and *submission* to God and His perfect will. As Eli said to Samuel, "He is the LORD; let him do what is good in his eyes" (1 Samuel 3:18; NIV).

I believe that if Rob could speak to us right now, he would remind us of those great people of faith remembered in the Book of Hebrews who "faced jeers and flogging, while still others were chained and put in prison. They were stoned; they were sawn in two; they were put to death by the sword. They went about in sheepskins and goatskins, destitute, persecuted and ill-treated" (Hebrews 11:36–37; NIV).

✝

These people now look down on us as "a great cloud of witnesses" to see how we will run this race of life (Hebrews 12:1). By faith, they all took their place in God's plan. Rob, in the normal course of events in this fallen world, was allowed to suffer a terrible disease . . . and has now joined their ranks. Will we choose to do the same?

QUESTIONS FOR GROUP DISCUSSION:

1. What situations can you think of that might push someone's faith to the breaking point?

2. What advice would you give a friend who is deeply wounded and broken due to suffering and/or death?

3. Read the account of Jesus in the Garden of Gethsemane in Matthew 26:36–44 and Luke 22:39–43. What principles can you gather from Jesus' words and actions that would be of help to someone facing great difficulty?

QUESTIONS FOR PERSONAL REFLECTION:

1. Spend some time alone with the Lord, asking Him to search your heart and reveal your ways (Psalm 139:23). In what ways do you need to "bend the knee" before Him as your sovereign Lord?

2. Carefully read John 15:4–5 and Philippians 4:11–14. How could you apply these verses in times when your faith is stretched thin?

BIBLE VERSES FOR CONTEMPLATION
AND MEMORIZATION:

Psalm 86
Matthew 11:28–30
Psalm 95:6–11

Endnotes
1. Philip Yancey, *Disappointment with God* (Grand Rapids, MI: Zondervan, 1988), p. 204.

CHAPTER EIGHT

Now, But Not Yet

I had been listening to Rob's sermon tape for about 40 minutes . . . and he was still on a roll. The fervency and the certainty with which he spoke painted an audible image of the brother I once had. It was very surreal. He sounded like the Rob that I knew; he sounded real, but I had to remind myself that the disease had by now taken almost everything that he had been when the sermon was recorded.

Rob had covered a lot of material in this one tape, and the message was saturated with vibrant passion, solid content, and practical application. He had covered the issues of sin, answering with solid biblical support the question that asked, "Why does suffering and death exist in a world with a good and loving God?" He had investigated the issues of physical healing and the "normal" course of human life in a fallen world . . . a course that included the inevitability of sickness, suffering, and death. He had expounded on the implications of Christ and the Cross, illuminating how that perfect sacrifice of God had paid the price for sin.

What a big difference when you can stand back and give people a big picture of history, I thought. When we understand the beauty and perfection of Eden, and how sin changed everything, we are forced to be consistent when we talk about good and bad, and right and wrong. Biblical history clearly brings each individual to a point where he or she must accept or reject the gospel. Each must either receive Christ's sacrifice and forgiveness, or turn away from Him for eternity. Wow. What a difference a truthful perspective makes. Rather than leading to fatalism and despair, believing in the history of Genesis gives us the foundation on which to build answers to these most probing of human issues.

I have seen many Christian leaders on television who have no solid answers to the questions surrounding death and suffering. They've said things like, "You just have to trust," or "You just have to have faith. We don't know why these things occurred." But you know why I believe that they can't give answers? It's because they don't believe the Book of Genesis. They don't believe God's Word as they should. They have been influenced *by* the world so they don't have this history that they can use to explain sin *to* the world. And so they can't give answers. It is only those who believe the history God has given to us (beginning in Genesis 1:1) who can consistently explain how there can be a loving God *and* death and suffering at the same time. As finite beings, we can't give ultimate and absolute answers in regard to everything, but we can give answers that are consistent, logical, rational, and defensible as we search the Scriptures for solutions.

As Rob tried to conclude his sermon on the tape, I smiled as he kept apologizing to the congregation because his message was going overtime. Yes, he was sorry — but not so sorry that he was willing to stop! He still had many things to say and was unable to restrain the words that were on his heart. They were words from the Word of God that could bring hope and eternal perspective to his church . . . and to us now years away from where he was. His passion for the Bible again overflowed as he turned his focus to the future. He began expounding on two things: first, the things that are reality in our lives *now*

✝

(now that we are in Christ); and second, the things that are *not yet* (the realities that await us on the other side of the grave when all things are made new again).

With his customary flair for words, he described the awkward balance in which we find ourselves as we navigate through life somewhere between "the Fall" and the coming "consummation" of history when Christ will return and all things will be restored. He had covered past history, explaining how we got to where we are in the present. Now he was explaining coming history, instructing how we are to move ahead, living out our place in the biblical "big picture" as it spans toward the future.

Now: Healed from Sin

I firmly believe that if Rob could talk to us today, he would tell us that he is restored and healed from the worst disease: sin. When Christ was on earth, He carried out great miracles, including wonderful physical healings of sick people. As significant as those individual healings were, Rob preached that "the Great Physician" had a broader focus of restoration in mind:

> When the Lord Jesus came, His whole purpose and reason was to pay the penalty for our sin, to appease the wrath of God, and to rise again from the dead. His whole purpose was to make us what He intends us to be. What does He intend us to be? Well, you see, He is speaking there about freedom

for the prisoners, sight for the blind, release of the oppressed. . . . It means this: He paid for our sins; He bought us forgiveness. That's what it's all about, real and genuine forgiveness so that He could bring us into a right relationship with God, with the Lord Jesus Christ.

Rob explained this further by expounding the passage in Isaiah 53:5 which states, "But He was wounded for our transgressions, He was bruised for our iniquities: the chastisement of our peace was upon Him, and by His stripes we are healed" (NKJV). Moving on to 1 Peter 2:22–24, he showed how this passage gives us the correct understanding of the Isaiah passage:

> He committed no sin, and no deceit was found in his mouth. When they hurled their insults at him, he did not retaliate; when he suffered, he made no threats. Instead, he entrusted himself to him who judges justly. He himself bore our sins in his body on the tree, so that we might die to sins and live for righteousness; by his wounds you have been healed (NIV).

As Rob preached on this particular passage, both the content of the passage and the importance of interpreting it properly became evident:

167

✟

What's the context here? That's what we have to examine. Let's put the Bible back in context, because a lot of people take verses out of context and they will just apply them to whatever they want. But the context here is this — that Peter is talking about the death of the Lord Jesus Christ for our sins. That's the whole emphasis and that's what he gets out of Isaiah 53. In fact, when it says "and by his wounds you have been healed," the Greek makes it clear that "you have been healed" is in the *passive* tense. It means you have *already* been healed.

Friends, you are all healed. The Bible tells us that if you are in the Lord Jesus Christ, Christ died to shed His blood so that you can be washed clean from your sin. That's the whole perspective of it. That's what it means. That's the context of it all. You *already have* been healed. You *already have* been washed clean from your sin.

You have been restored to Christ, and it's *now and not yet*. Now we have the cleansing and forgiveness. Yet to come is a new heaven and new earth in which there will be no sicknesses and no death. But the primary emphasis is definitely not on physical healing now. Our primary focus here is on the Lord Jesus Christ and His death and resurrection for us. That's what that verse means.

In fact, we know that the Lord Jesus went out and healed people; He went out casting out evil spirits; He went out raising people from the dead. . . . He did that. He stopped the storm, didn't He? Remember that? In all of this, the Lord Jesus is showing us that our restoration is to be spiritual. That's what He is talking about, that's what He is showing us. That our restoration is spiritual now. *Right now.* Right now, you and I, through the Lord Jesus Christ, are spiritually restored to God. *Right now*, through the Lord Jesus, through His death and His resurrection. But you see, it is *now and not yet.* It is yet to come. . . . We are living in a world where we are living *now and not yet.* Now we are spiritually restored to God, spiritually restored through the Lord Jesus Christ, yes, but it is yet to come.

What is yet to come? What is yet to come is a new heaven and a new earth. That is what we are looking forward to. And in fact, that is where our focus needs to be, friends, because in the new heaven and the new earth the Lord Jesus, who *is* righteousness, will dwell there, and we shall dwell with Him. Isn't that fantastic? We don't want to focus on this world; it's a world ruined by sin. We don't want to focus on ourselves; we are people who have been ruined by sin. We want to focus on the new heaven and the new earth that is yet to come. . . . In that new heaven and new earth, there will be no sickness; there will be no disease; there will be no demons; there will be no death; there will be no chaos. . . . Everything is going to be peaceful and perfect. Wonderful, isn't it? You see, now and not yet. Restored to Christ today, yes — and yet to come is all that we are looking forward to in the new heaven and the new earth.

In fact, you see the New Testament emphasis is not primarily on physical healing, but it is on the power of the Holy Spirit who brings us into a right relationship with the Lord Jesus Christ. That is the primary aspect of the New Testament.

Right now, this spiritual healing from sin is about relationship, a trusting relationship that is more valuable than anything else on earth. Paul put this into words in Philippians 3:8–10:

> More than that, I count all things to be loss in view of the surpassing value of knowing Christ Jesus my Lord, for whom I have suffered the loss of all things, and count them but rubbish so that I may gain Christ, and may be found in Him, not having a righteousness of my own derived

from the Law, but that which is through faith in Christ, the righteousness which comes from God on the basis of faith, that I may know Him and the power of His resurrection and the fellowship of His sufferings, being conformed to His death (NAS95).

That relationship starts at the moment Christ comes into our spirits and is cultivated until death. As Rob said, it is *now, but not yet.* Yet to come is the final consummation of all things, a complete and total healing for the soul and the body and the world that ushers in a new and never-ending era of unhindered intimacy with the Creator. "Now we see in a mirror dimly, but then face to face," says 1 Corinthians 13:12.

The Bible tells us that sometime in the future we will see a restoring of the harmony that existed in Eden once again. For example, Isaiah 11:6 says:

And the wolf will dwell with the lamb, and the leopard will lie down with the kid, and the calf and the young lion and the fatling together; and a little boy will lead them.

In peace they will exist together, apparently as vegetarians again. You have a little child. You have a viper . . . and they're not frightened of each other; they won't

✝

harm each other. And you know what equates to that situation? Righteousness and restoration. Acts 3:18–21 speaks of this restoration and where it fits in the big picture:

> But the things which God announced beforehand by the mouth of all the prophets, that His Christ would suffer, He has thus fulfilled. Repent therefore and return, that your sins may be wiped away, in order that times of refreshing may come from the presence of the Lord; and that He may send Jesus, the Christ appointed for you, whom heaven must receive until the period of restoration of all things about which God spoke by the mouth of His holy prophets from ancient time.

Note that God is going to *restore* and He is going to make all things new *again.* The standard to which we will return is the one that existed so long ago in Eden. Everything will be in balance once again — the groaning of creation will cease and the righteousness that is equated with peace and harmony with the animals and man will be the norm again, just as it was before sin.

Might I ask, however, where we would be without this foundation of hope? From Genesis we are able to see the picture of how things were, telling us also of how they will be. Only from the perfection of the past can we tangibly hope in the promise of this glorious future. Those who reject a literal Genesis have little to go on, and will probably never understand the believer's hope — the hope that life will again be as perfect as it once was, but no longer is. How can there be a restoration to such a perfect state when there never was one to start with? Without this understanding there is no longing for heaven, a grim outlook on life, lack of true joy, and the beginning of a steady slide into spiritual bankruptcy and lukewarmness.

The existence of Eden, as long ago as it was, gives hope for the future. Between now and then, in a world where death and sin are "normal," this hope gives us faith to face another day. I believe we are incapable of imagining what heaven will be like, just as we are unable to truly imagine what life was like in Eden before the Fall. We do know that there will be no Curse (Revelation 22:3). In this present sin-cursed world, we live in sin-ravaged bodies that cause us to groan. But what an encouragement to know that Christ will one day restore our bodies, and the whole creation, to perfection!

We see a glimpse of the complete healing of all creation that will take place through the ministry of Christ and the Apostles. Of course, we wish this would happen now — and at times, for His purposes, God does ordain specific miraculous events to overcome the consequences of the Curse. But at the right time, God will bring this present era to a close, this great season of suffering and death will end — and then, for all those who do trust in Him, we will have that final healing. Yes, we have a fraction of it *now*, but the completeness of it is *not yet*.

Between Now and Then

Therefore be careful how you walk, not as unwise men but as wise, making the most of your time, because the days are evil. So then do not be foolish, but understand what the will of the Lord is (Ephesians 5:15–16).

Living as we are now (between "the Fall" and "the consummation"), how then should we live? In the above verse, Paul challenges us to live lives of wisdom and careful progression. These would be lives that are lived in *truth, trust,* and with a vision for *eternity*.

John 8:32 says, "You shall know the truth, and the truth shall make you free." This certainly is the case when dealing with origins and the big picture of biblical history (including a proper understanding of Eden, the Fall, Christ, and the Cross, and the restoration that will consummate all things). The truth about inevitability of death sets us free as well. Because of what we know through the revealed Word of God, we no longer need to be bound by the fear of death. Having received the gospel, we can even be expectant and looking forward to what lies beyond the grave. Where do we find such truth? Jesus himself is truth (John 14:6), and the Bible, we must always remember, is truth as well (Psalm 119:160). Devotion to its study and upholding its authority is central to living a life of wisdom.

> The grass withers, the flower fades, when the breath of the LORD blows upon it; surely the people are grass. The grass withers, the flower fades, but the word of our God stands forever (Isaiah 40:7–8).

A life of wisdom is also built on trust. We are to trust in God as the Creator and sustainer of all existence, trust in His immediate presence in our lives, and trust in His continued provision as we seek to live lives of faith in the midst of suffering and death.

> But he said to me, "My grace is sufficient for you, for my power is made perfect in weakness." Therefore I will boast all the more gladly about my weaknesses, so that Christ's power may rest on me. That is why, for Christ's sake, I delight in weaknesses, in insults, in hardships, in persecutions, in difficulties. For when I am weak then I am strong (2 Corinthians 12:9–10; NIV).

Wisdom dictates that you not only trust in Him, but that you also trust in who the Scriptures say you now are *in Christ*. Between now and death, it will always be a challenge to remember that the very presence of God is not just *with* you, but is *within* you (John 14:17). Continually, you will need to renew your minds according to the biblical fact that you have been crucified with Him and it is no longer you who live, but Christ who lives in you (Galatians 2:20). When it is time to submit and obey, you must be wise to recognize that God's Spirit himself gives you the power and the desire to do what is right (John 15:5; Philippians 4:13).

Again, in those times when wisdom fails and circumstances tear at your heart . . . when the tears will not cease and the grief will not lift . . . in those times there will always be the need to bow the knee before God as your only sovereign King and trust Him in spite of all that you see and all that you feel. Then you can make wise and godly decisions in this fallen world. We read in Deuteronomy 30:19–20 how the Israelites were offered a choice by God; it's the same choice that you have day by day:

> I call heaven and earth to witness against you today, that I have set before you life and death, the blessing and the curse. So choose life in order that you may live, you and your descendants, by

loving the LORD your God, by obeying His voice, and by holding fast to Him.

Finally, wisdom requires a vision for eternity. We simply must accept the reality of our mortality and live lives for the things that will never end. The Bible tells us something that science knows very well. "The length of our days is seventy years — or eighty, if we have the strength; yet their span is but trouble and sorrow, for they quickly pass, and we fly away" (Psalm 90:10; NIV). We consider someone who lives to 80 years old to have had a long life. However, contemplate this: *How long is 80 compared to eternity?* Job 8:9 says, "We were born only yesterday and know nothing, and our days on earth are but a shadow" (NIV). Even though we live in time (and to us the sufferings of a loved one like Rob seem so prolonged), compared to eternity it's not even a fleeting moment. That does not in any way negate the trauma of it all in this life, but we do need to put it all in perspective and try to see more of the "big picture" as God has revealed it in the Bible.

Suffering and death from sin is the universal norm, and that should be a warning to us — a reminder that our days are numbered. If we are wise, we will invest the best of all our resources for things with eternal significance.

✦

Do not store up for yourselves treasures on earth, where moth and rust destroy, and where thieves break in and steal. But store up for yourselves treasures in heaven, where moth and rust do not destroy, and where thieves do not break in and steal. For where your treasure is, there your your heart will be also (Matthew 6:19–21; NIV).

Lift up your eyes to the sky, then look to the earth beneath; for the sky will vanish like smoke, and the earth will wear out like a garment, and its inhabitants will die in like manner. But My salvation shall be forever, and my righteousness shall not wane (Isaiah 51:6).

How important it is to put our trust in the living and inerrant Word of God and live for worthy purposes. Think about this! Eventually, you *will* die for what you are living for, since eventually, you will die. It's not a matter of *if* you will die (we know that is a certainty). It's a matter of living for a cause that is worth dying for.

For truly I say to you, until heaven and earth pass away, not the smallest letter or stroke shall pass away from the Law, until all is accomplished (Matthew 5:18).

For I do not consider my life of any account as dear to myself, in order that I may finish my course, and the ministry which I received from the Lord Jesus, to testify solemnly of the gospel of the grace of God (Acts 20:24).

From Genesis to Revelation

In the beginning, we know that God created the heavens and the earth, and then man and woman. When He was done, He said it was all exceptionally good. Sin has polluted it all, but still a remnant remains . . . a shattered reflection of the pure good that once was. We can still see the beauty in nature and in art. Even human love (as conditional and fickle as it is) can be a tainted remnant of the perfect, unconditional love of God and a reminder of the way things used to be in the Garden before sin. In the song *Echoes of Eden*, Stephen Curtis Chapman sings about human love, and how it is a shadow of the pure intimacy we once had (and will have again) with our Creator:

> What is it about a kiss that makes me feel like this?
> What is it that makes my heart beat faster when I'm in your arms?
> What is it about your touch that amazes me so much?

✠

How is it that your sweet smile can get me through the hardest mile?

What's the magic in your eyes that brings the love in me alive?

What is it about this dance, the sweetness of our romance — that makes me feel this way?

These are the echoes of Eden,
Reflections of what we were created for
Hints of the passion and freedom
That waits on the other side of heaven's door.
These are the echoes of Eden.

How is it the sky turns gray anytime you're far away?

What is it that makes me sad anytime you're feeling bad?

What is it about this night, the music and the candlelight,

That makes me feel this way?

These are the echoes of Eden,
Reflections of what we were created for.
Hints of the passion and freedom
That waits on the other side of heaven's door.
These are the echoes of Eden.

What is it about this night, the music, and the candlelight that makes me feel this way?

These are the echoes of Eden,
Reflections of what we were created for.
Hints of the passion and freedom
That waits on the other side of heaven's door.
These are the echoes of Eden.

Between Eden and the new heaven and the new earth, we will live for an unknown duration of time. In the Book of Revelation, chapters 21 and 22, God gives the apostle John a vision for what will emerge from the disease, destruction, and death of the present days. The descriptions paint a picture of the future that awaits us. Both the parallels and the contrast between what once was and what will be are important:

> . . . and He shall dwell among them, and they shall be His people, and God Himself shall be among them, and He shall wipe away every tear from their eyes; and there shall no longer be any death; there shall no longer be any mourning, or crying, or pain; the first things have passed away (Revelation 21:3–4).

✝ And he showed me a river of the water of life, clear as crystal, coming from the throne of God and of the Lamb, in the middle of its street. And on either side of the river was the tree of life, bearing twelve kinds of fruit, yielding its fruit every month; and the leaves of the tree were for the healing of the nations (Revelation 22:1–2).

The new heaven and the new earth: This is the great hope for all who suffer in this fallen world. This is the hope God leaves us in the closing chapters of the Bible . . . and this is the hope that Rob left his congregation at the end of his sermon. As I turned off the tape, I realized that he had recorded this sermon only a few months before "frontal lobe dementia" began to make him an extreme illustration to his own message.

The Last "Goodbye"

The last time I saw my brother alive, I sat beside his bed watching my mother lovingly caress his head. "I wish he could just say 'Mum' one more time," she said. Instead there were times when her son (obviously not knowing what he was doing) would push her away — seemingly to reject the loving hand that gently stroked his cheek.

Unmoved, our mother continued to patiently feed him his favorite drinks, instinctively hoping to satisfy his hunger, perhaps giving him some joy and comfort — if he could even experience such feelings in his embattled state.

I looked on with mixed emotion. On the one hand, I wanted to cry. On the other hand, I rejoiced that Rob already had the most important healing of all. His spiritual healing from sin meant when he passed away from this earth, he would be totally healed in eternity. Many memories and many Bible verses passed though my mind in those final minutes with him:

> For I consider that the sufferings of this present time are not worthy to be compared with the glory which shall be revealed to us (Romans 8:18).

> For our light and momentary troubles are achieving for us an eternal glory that far outweighs them all (2 Corinthians 4:17; NIV).

Knowing that this would probably be my final goodbye to Robert, I bent over and kissed him on his forehead. "Goodbye, Robert. I love you, brother," I said. I left the room holding back tears, but also departed with a real peace — the kind of peace "which surpasses all comprehension" (Philippians 4:7). The tears would come, and then come again and again. Even today, I can't think about him for very long without feeling the loss and reliving portions of the pain. . . . But those emotions I know will one day cease as well, as every tear is wiped away by Jesus . . . this I know, for the Bible says it's so. The question has been answered through the big picture of God's Holy Word. *Why is there suffering and death?* Eden was lost to sin. I now live in a fallen world. But in the future there will be a restoration and a healing that is beyond the imagination. In the meantime, I know that my brother is in the hands of His Creator, as I am . . . now, but not yet.

I held my mother closely as we walked down the hallway, out the door of the nursing home, and toward the car. Around us, people continued about their daily business, boarding buses, coming out of stores with armloads of goods, children laughing on their way home from school. . . . it all looked so normal in the bright sunlight. People were going to and fro, indifferent and unaware of what was happening to my brother Robert. But why should they? They didn't know him or know what was happening to him. Why should they care?

But as I looked at them, I thought of the fact that each one of them is, like Rob, going to face death one day. Many of them will end up in nursing homes, aimlessly staring at the wall, their minds tragically deteriorated from the effects of disease. What is the purpose of all that they are doing now if death is just the end of it all? Is it all, in the end, futility? No, no it's not.

In fact, it is all full of meaning, guided by the hand of the God who not only created it all, but also causes it all to work together for good — and soon enough He will restore it all once again. We all will die, yes, but we all will live for eternity either in heaven (the renewed creation) with our Creator, or in hell, separated from Him for eternity.

As I thought about this, I felt anew Robert's passion and the burden he felt to warn the world about the true meaning of life and tell them the wonderful saving message of the gospel. *That's what Rob would want me to feel,* I thought. They need to care — they need to face the reality of death. At the car with my mother, I thought about the fact that one day I'll have to say goodbye to her also . . . and the fact that I too will someday finish my days on this earth. Until then, suffering and death will be the norm. But after that. . . .

> There shall no longer be any curse; and the throne of God and of the Lamb shall be in it, and His bond-servants shall serve Him; they shall see His face, and His name shall be on their foreheads. And there shall no longer be any night; and they shall not have need of the light of a lamp nor the light of the sun, because the Lord God shall illumine them; and they shall reign forever and ever (Revelation 22:3–5).

✝

He who testifies to these things says, "Yes, I am coming quickly." Amen. Come, Lord Jesus. The grace of the Lord Jesus be with all. Amen (Revelation 22:20–21).

QUESTIONS FOR GROUP DISCUSSION:

1. In Philippians 3:8–10, Paul said that knowing Christ was more important than all other things. Review this passage. Would you agree or disagree with him? Give solid reasons for your answer.

2. If someone does not believe history as it is recorded in Genesis, how might that affect their hope for the future as prophesied in Revelation? Do you think someone can hope in heaven without an understanding of Eden? Why or why not?

3. When it comes to living wisely and making the most of our days, do you think it is more important to have truth, trust, or a vision for eternity?

QUESTIONS FOR PERSONAL REFLECTION:

1. Find a quiet place where you can pray and read God's Word without interruption. Skim back through the many passages of Scripture we have discussed in this book, and review any notes you have from the group

discussions, the personal reflections, and the verses for contemplation and memorization. Then read James 1:22–25. How do you think God wants to change your life in light of all that He has shown you through the Bible?

BIBLE VERSES FOR CONTEMPLATION AND MEMORIZATION:

2 Corinthians 1:3–7
1 Peter 1:6–16

EPILOGUE

BY STEPHEN HAM

When Job's three friends, Eliphaz the Temanite, Bildad the Shuhite and Zophar the Naamathite, heard about all the troubles that had come upon him, they set out from their homes and met together by agreement to go and sympathize with him and comfort him. When they saw him from a distance, they could hardly recognize him; they began to weep aloud, and they tore their robes and sprinkled dust on their heads. Then they sat on the ground with him for seven days and seven nights. No one said a word to him because they saw how great his suffering was (Job 2:11–13; NIV).

We often only hear about Job's three friends in a negative light. From chapter 4 to 37 of the Book of Job, we find numerous accounts of these men accusing Job of sin or making erroneous assumptions about the cause of Job's suffering. What happened for them to go so far off track? For the first seven days, Eliphaz, Bildad, and Zophar simply sat with Job, not saying a word and supporting him in his suffering. Job had three fantastic friends, right up to the point where they decided to open their mouths. Then everything went downhill.

Before I start accusing Job's friends of their insensitivities, perhaps I should have a good look in the mirror. Perhaps we all should. I can certainly testify to being like Job's friends. With all sincere intentions from family and friends in supporting my sister-in-law and her family through the suffering of my brother Rob, we would all have to admit that we made mistakes in helping them.

Whether it is incorrect assumptions or unhelpful statements or something else, every human being needs to understand how easy it can be to hurt those who are already hurting. Stressful situations, such as watching a loved one suffer, can bring out the worst in us if we are not careful. I have learned that we need to be on a careful self-watch for this.

The one thing it does highlight, however, is that we are again burdened by limitations. Just as Job's friends were limited in their understanding of why Job was going through his suffering, we are also limited in our understanding of each individual tragedy. Sometimes it is best for us to simply be like Job's friends in the first seven days and just be there. Sure, we can provide a meal, transport, and moral support, or any other practical need, and we should. When it comes time to open our mouths, however, perhaps we should consider very carefully whether it really needs to be said and whether our mortal limitations have hindered our insight.

The ongoing frustration of living as limited beings is the frustration of mystery. We have learned by reading this book that the basis for all suffering is original sin. Yes, we do live in a sin-corrupted and cursed world, but beyond this fact there is also mystery. Just as Job and his friends did not have the insight to know about the satanic affliction Job was suffering and just as my family will never really know for sure about what caused Rob's illness, we will all be left with many unanswered questions.

It is in these times that we should stick to the facts. Hopefully the foundational facts have been made overwhelmingly clear as you have read through the pages of this book. The facts clearly point to an all-powerful Creator, a perfect original creation, and a rebellious human race that caused that creation to be cursed by our sin. While our sin caused a corrupted creation, our God remains incorruptible. It is because of this that we turn to Him in acceptance of His infinite wisdom for the other questions that will remain unanswered in our lifetime in this world. The one thing we can all know is that the effect of sin is indiscriminate and every human being will likely face death. But not every human being will face death.

✞

Through James (the brother of Jesus), God has given us some great teaching in helping us to bear the load of suffering and turmoil we have in this world as His children.

In James 5:7 we read, "Be patient, therefore, brethren, until the coming of the Lord." Whether our suffering is at the hands of others or due to something inexplicable, those who have come to faith in Jesus Christ can be hopeful of a wonderful future. James tells us that the Lord is coming. One day, maybe sooner than we realize, Jesus will come again to this world just as He left it. He will come in triumph and final judgement. We may be the ones that witness His final consummation and, depending on your relationship with Christ, this becomes either a hopeful anticipation or a terrible dread.

The truth is, my brother Rob has faced death prior to the second coming of Christ. He is now healed in the presence of Christ for eternity. One day, everyone who has experienced salvation in Jesus Christ will be healed, and yet even this is not the greatest reason to look forward to being in heaven. Something even greater awaits us in heaven than healing.

The Presence of God

Can you imagine an eternity in the presence of God unhindered by any limitation of sin placed on our relationship with Him? What a glorious existence that will be. We don't deserve it, but He is giving it anyway. This is the greatest "why" question. It is the question that we will leave you asking and we will let you ask it in the words of one of the greatest hymns ever written.

And Can It Be That I Should Gain?

And can it be that I should gain
An interest in the Savior's blood?
Died He for me, who caused His pain —
For me, who Him to death pursued?
Amazing love! How can it be,
That thou, my God, shouldst die for me?
Amazing love! How can it be,
That Thou, my God, shouldst die for me?

'Tis mystery all: th' Immortal dies:
Who can explore His strange design?
In vain the firstborn seraph tries
To sound the depths of love divine.
'Tis mercy all! Let earth adore,
Let angel minds inquire no more.
'Tis mercy all! Let earth adore;
Let angel minds inquire no more.

He left His Father's throne above
So free, so infinite His grace —

✠

Emptied himself of all but love,
And bled for Adam's helpless race:
'Tis mercy all, immense and free,
For O my God, it found out me!
'Tis mercy all, immense and free,
For O my God, it found out me!

Long my imprisoned spirit lay,
Fast bound in sin and nature's night;
Thine eye diffused a quickening ray —
I woke, the dungeon flamed with light;
My chains fell off, my heart was free,
I rose, went forth, and followed Thee.
My chains fell off, my heart was free,
I rose, went forth, and followed Thee.

Still the small inward voice I hear,
That whispers all my sins forgiven;
Still the atoning blood is near,
That quenched the wrath of hostile heaven.
I feel the life His wounds impart;
I feel the Savior in my heart.
I feel the life His wounds impart;
I feel the Savior in my heart.

No condemnation now I dread;
Jesus, and all in Him, is mine;

Alive in Him, my living Head,
And clothed in righteousness divine,
Bold I approach th' eternal throne,
And claim the crown, through Christ my own.
Bold I approach th' eternal throne,
And claim the crown, through Christ my own.

(Words by Charles Wesley)

RESOURCES

DeYoung, Don. *Thousands Not Billions*. Green Forest, AR: Master Books, 2005.

Edwards, Brian. *Nothing but the Truth*. Darlington, UK: Evangelical Press, 1993.

Ham, Ken, Jason Lisle, and Terry Mortenson. Answers Academy Curriculum. Hebron, KY: Answers in Genesis.

Ham, Ken. *The Great Dinosaur Mystery Solved*. Green Forest, AR: Master Books, 1998.

Ham, Ken. *The Lie: Evolution*. Green Forest, AR: Master Books, 1987.

Ham, Ken. *The New Answers Book*. Green Forest, AR: Master Books, 2007.

Ham, Ken, and others. *War of the Worldviews*. Green Forest, AR: Master Books, 2005.

Humber, Paul G. *Evolution Exposed*. Enumclaw, WA: Pleasant Word, 2006.

Humphreys, D. Russell. *Starlight and Time*. Green Forest, AR: Master Books, 1994.

Jones, Floyd Nolen. *The Chronology of the Old Testament*. Green Forest, AR: Master Books, 2004.

Lubenow, Marvin L. *Bones of Contention*. Grand Rapids, MI: Baker Books, 2004.

Morris, Henry. *The Genesis Record*. Grand Rapids, MI: Baker Book House, 1976.

Morris, John D. *The Young Earth*. Green Forest, AR: Master Books, 2004.

Mortenson, Terry. *The Great Turning Point*. Green Forest, AR: Master Books, 2004.

Oard, Mike. *Frozen in Time*. Green Forest, AR: Master Books, 2004.

Parker, Gary. *Creation: Facts of Life*. Green Forest, AR: Master Books, revised 2006.

Ussher, James. *The Annals of the World*. Green Forest, AR: Master Books, 2003.

Woodmorappe, John. *Noah's Ark: A Feasibility Study*. Santee, CA: Institute for Creation Research, 2004.

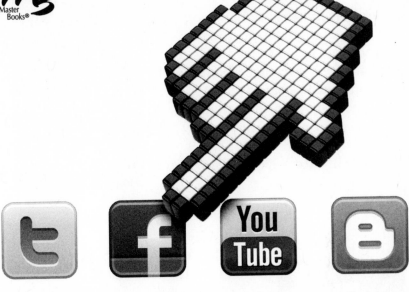

Connect with Master Books®

masterbooks.net

An imprint of New Leaf Publishing Group

facebook.com/**masterbooks**
twitter.com/**masterbooks4u**
youtube.com/**nlpgvideo**

nlpgblogs.com
nlpgvideos.com

join us at **Creation**Conversations.com

FOR FURTHER READING

THE LIE: EVOLUTION
Ken Ham

This is the most powerful message for Christians witnessing to this generation — easy to read and meaningful to everyone who reads it. Completely debunks the myth of evolution. Junior high to adult.

paperback • 190 pages • $10.99
ISBN-13: 978-0-89051-158-9
ISBN-10: 0-89051-158-6

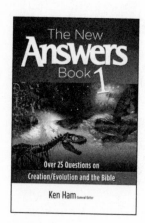

THE NEW ANSWERS BOOK 1
Ken Ham, General Editor

In today's world, Christians find challenges to their faith every day. This new resource from Answers in Genesis gives answers for some of the most difficult questions that modern Christians face. An impressive list of reputable creation scientists joins author Ken Ham to answer the top 25 questions on creation/evolution scientifically, biblically, and logically. Christians of all ages face challenges to their faith from those who emphasize evolution and millions-of-years thinking. This resource will provide you with a ready answer!

paperback • 360 pages • $14.99
ISBN-13: 978-0-89051-509-9
ISBN-10: 0-89051-509-3

AVAILABLE AT CHRISTIAN BOOKSTORES NATIONWIDE

FOR FURTHER READING

RAISING GODLY CHILDREN IN AN UNGODLY WORLD
Ken Ham and Steve Ham

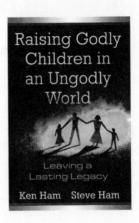

People often mistakenly get caught up in the idea of leaving a financial inheritance for their children instead of the true responsibility of raising children to love God first and foremost. Ignoring the common focus of a traditional inheritance, Ken and Steve reveal a powerful vision for leaving a legacy of faith for future generations.

paper • 240 pages • $12.99
ISBN-13: 978-0-89051-542-6
ISBN-10: 0-89051-542-6

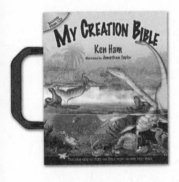

MY CREATION BIBLE
Ken Ham

My Creation Bible takes children on an important journey of faith and biblical history, from when God created everything to the importance of Christ and the cross. It includes bright, colorful, precious illustrations with a sensitive portrayal of biblical truths. Features a die cut cover, with a unique carrying handle. From Eden to the ark and beyond, children will love to not only read it, but also take it with them to share with friends! Includes a great CD musical version of the text.

board book • 11 spreads • $11.99
ISBN-13: 978-0-89051-462-7
ISBN-10: 0-89051-462-3

AVAILABLE AT CHRISTIAN BOOKSTORES NATIONWIDE

CREATION MUSEUM
Prepare to believe.

The Creation Museum presents a fully engaging "walk through history." Designed by a former Universal Studios exhibit director, this state-of-the-art 70,000 square foot museum brings the pages of the Bible to life with realistic murals and scenery, computer-generated visual effects, dozens of exotic animals and life-sized people, and dinosaur animatronics. Our special-effects theater, complete with misty sea breezes and rumbling seats, adds adventure to family-sized fun, right from the beginning!

For ticket and exhibit information, please visit us at
creationmuseum.org.

For Further Information

Answers in Genesis ministries are evangelical, Christ-centered, non-denominational, and non-profit.

Answers in Genesis
P.O. Box 510
Hebron, KY 41048
USA

Answers in Genesis
P.O. Box 5262
Leicester LE2 3XU
United Kingdom

In addition, you may contact:

Institute for Creation Research
P.O. Box 2667
El Cajon, CA 92021